CÁNTICO

A Selection

Jorge Guillén

Jorge Guillén devoted thirty-one years to the writing of CÁNTICO. He himself made the choice of the fifty original poems for this volume and also contributed the introduction. He has received a number of international awards and prizes, among them two Guggenheim Fellowships and the Grand Prix International de Poésie at the Fifth Biennial of Knokke–Le Zoute, Belgium. Guillén was appointed Charles Eliot Norton Professor of Poetry at Harvard University for 1957–1958. He has taught in Europe at the Sorbonne and at Oxford as well as at the Universities of Murcia and Seville; he arrived in America in 1938 and was Professor at Wellesley College from 1940 until his retirement in 1957.

Norman Thomas di Giovanni edited the volume largely in collaboration with the author. He has published translations of Spanish and Italian verse in various magazines and anthologies. His own work (prose) has appeared in the *Nation,* the *Atlantic* and the *New Republic.*

The poems in English are the work of the following translator-poets: Ben Belitt, Alastair Reid, Richard Wilbur, Mark Strand, Stephen Berg, W. S. Merwin, Hubert Creekmore, James Wright, Barbara Howes and Alan Dugan.

JORGE GUILLÉN

Cántico

A Selection

EDITED BY

NORMAN THOMAS DI GIOVANNI

An Atlantic Monthly Press Book

LITTLE, BROWN AND COMPANY · BOSTON · TORONTO

LIBRARY OF CONGRESS CATALOG CARD NO. 64-10955

FIRST EDITION

Spanish text originally published by Editorial Sudamericana,
Buenos Aires. Copyright 1950 by Jorge Guillén.
The author and editor wish to thank the following for per-
mission to include copyrighted material: Harcourt, Brace
and World, Inc., and Faber & Faber, Ltd., for Richard Wil-
bur's translations, "The Horses" and "Death, from a
Distance," from *Advice to a Prophet and Other Poems* by
Richard Wilbur. © 1959, 1961 by Richard Wilbur.

ATLANTIC-LITTLE, BROWN BOOKS
ARE PUBLISHED BY
LITTLE, BROWN AND COMPANY
IN ASSOCIATION WITH
THE ATLANTIC MONTHLY PRESS

*Published simultaneously in Canada
by Little, Brown & Company (Canada) Limited*

PRINTED IN GREAT BRITAIN

THE TRANSLATORS

Ben Belitt
Stephen Berg
Hubert Creekmore
Norman Thomas di Giovanni
Alan Dugan
Barbara Howes
W. S. Merwin
Alastair Reid
Mark Strand
Richard Wilbur
James Wright

CONTENTS

EDITOR'S NOTE

The Spanish originals of the fifty poems in this volume were chosen by Jorge Guillén himself. The idea that guided the selection was to distill from the more than three hundred poems of the complete book an essential *Cántico*, an edition representing all of the book's various elements: its chief subjects and themes, its different verse forms and poem lengths. And as an extra measure a large proportion of the important longer poems was included. The author's introduction, the chronology of his life and work, and the poems in English (except for two which appeared together in a magazine before this book was projected) were specially prepared for the present edition. Poets made the translations, asked by the editor only to create a poem in English satisfactory to themselves and to him. Along the way Guillén looked over and gave his approval to the poems, but responsibility for them rests solely with the editor working with each poet-translator.

The form of the complete *Cántico* is a result of its careful development through several editions. While writing his poems for each successive enlargement, Guillén at the same time prepared – literally made – his book, designing and arranging his poems for the eventual printed page. And so in this selected edition the over-all symmetry of the full text has been followed, and certain of the visual aspects of the original – not just Guillén's presence on the page but his presence *over* the page – have been adhered to. (This explains the use of three different type sizes in the poem titles: a regular type size for most of the poems, but a larger type for the major poems and a smaller type for the minor.) An attempt has been made, in this way, both to keep faith with the whole work and to give the reader a better sense of it.

INTRODUCTION

by Jorge Guillén

I

The author of these poems looks back on himself as a member not of any literary school, but rather of a literary generation. That generation, which grew together into a living community, made no attempt to reduce itself to a system. Rarely has there been such a clear harmony of belief as there was in the tastes and objectives of those young men, whose intellectual life centered in Madrid during the twenties. If we accept Ortega y Gasset's definition of a generation as a group of men born within a fifteen-year span, our generation would take 1898 as its central date, for in that year were born Federico García Lorca, Dámaso Alonso and Vicente Aleixandre. A little older than them were Pedro Salinas, Gerardo Diego and myself; a little younger were Emilio Prados, Luis Cernuda, Rafael Alberti and Manuel Altolaguirre. (This enumeration is unjustly – but necessarily – incomplete.)

For the most part these poets were Andalusians. Castile and Andalusia have always been the main sources of Spanish poetry, with Castile predominant in the past and Andalusia today. All of us Castilians and Andalusians turned out to be, quite unintentionally, as up-to-date as our contemporaries in Europe and America. Our strongest feelings were in tune with the general atmosphere of the twenties, though at the same time we echoed a purely Spanish tradition.

Bear in mind this characteristic of tradition. That "avant-garde" generation, as it was then called, had no need to disavow any of its predecessors in order to assert itself. As Dámaso Alonso said, "that generation was not in revolt against anything." Our roots were sunk deep in the Golden Age, the so-called *Siglo de Oro,* and not in Góngora alone. Just as we reclaimed for our own don Luis of Córdoba, we read and reread with the same love Garcilaso, Gil Vicente, San Juan de la Cruz, Lope de Vega and Quevedo. All the poets of our generation held this interest in common, not only those of us (Pedro Salinas, Gerardo Diego, Dámaso Alonso and myself) who took up teaching. Ancient and modern works were admired whenever they promoted *genuineness* in poetry. For that reason Bécquer was also studied and championed. Among our immediate masters – and admired above all – were Antonio Machado and Juan Ramón Jiménez. The most widely read and best-loved of foreign poets were the French, from Baudelaire to the surrealists.

Friendship was the link among us all. And the dominant note of our relations to our predecessors and older contemporaries was also one of harmony. It was a harmony of even greater significance because it evolved on the eve of the terrible civil war that was to break out in 1936. Though politically we were not militants, neither did we ignore politics, for we were decidedly in favor

2

of a more open Spain. There have been individuals who have somewhat obtusely called the generation of Salinas and his friends "the generation of the Dictatorship," but none of us participated in any way in the regime of Primo de Rivera, whose dictatorship was so unmodern that it made no attempt to control either our behavior or our writings. Between 1920 and 1936 we were relatively free – free to fulfill our individual destinies. The writers of the dictatorship came later.

We poets got along well together, yet at the same time were very different from each other. How, then, can one designate in a single phrase those fruitful years between the two world wars? There is no fitting label. *Aire de época*, the identity of an age, does not mean a "group style." Yet there were certain characteristics that we all admired. Reality *represented*, not depicted according to a specific likeness. Reality, not realism. And sentiment – without which there is no poetry – stripped of gesticulation. Sentiment, not sentimentality, which we condemned as the vilest of obscenities.

But because of our restraint in the show of emotions, some of us were judged cold, even though we were passionately dedicated to voicing our enthusiasm for the world, our commitment to life, our love of love. Were we cold, abstract, intellectual? We may have been a little difficult, perhaps, but not overly so. We were all of us speaking in images. And on this ground – the reliance on metaphor – our threads came together. The American label "imagists" could be applied to any of the writers of imagination who were working on either side of the Atlantic during the twenties. This cult of the image was the common denominator among the apparently contradictory forms that were debated by the poets of those years, and not just the Spanish poets.

On the other hand, we felt the word "poetry" in its fullest connotation. To understand the atmosphere of those years, one must grasp this will to poetry as creation, this acceptance of the poem as the world in quintessence. And what if the poem itself turned out to be our whole theory of poetry? It was necessary to identify to the highest possible degree poetry and poem. However, even this was not an organized doctrine. Of "isms" there were only two: *creacionismo*, whose founder was the admirable Chilean poet Vicente Huidobro and whose followers were Juan Larrea and Gerardo Diego; and surrealism, which was in effect an invitation to untrammeled imagination. But whatever our route, our aspiration was that the poem should be, word by word, image by image, intensely poetic.

II

Not having been precocious, I was twenty-five when I began writing. It was in Paris in 1918. Why had I never written before that? Because I never dared. But from time to time I would say to my friends, "I'd give anything to write a book of verse!" Even then I was thinking about a single work with an organic unity. The rigorous form

4

of *Les Fleurs du Mal* fascinated me, and later on I discovered *Leaves of Grass*.

My *annus mirabilis* was 1919. That summer, on a beach in Brittany (at Tregastel), a book began taking shape that was to be called *Cántico* when it appeared in Madrid nine years later. In that first edition there were seventy-five poems; but little by little the book kept growing, until the complete edition – the fourth, with three hundred and thirty-four poems – was published in Buenos Aires in 1950. It was in the peace and freedom of Wellesley, Massachusetts, that many of these poems were written.

The slow, almost continuous work of writing *Cántico* moved forward spontaneously, impelled in a constant direction. Each poem flowed from the same source but followed its own inclination. The poems were related to one another only from within. Nothing was ever plotted; there was always freedom to pursue an impulse. In this way a spontaneous unity, one that was neither artificial nor imposed from without, began to dominate the work long before the architectonic unity into which thirty-one years' writing finally settled. Out of this organic unity there had to come a book that was truly a book and not just an album of poems. Each unforeseen line of verse was directed consciously or unconsciously toward a single goal. The subject matter, however, was drawn from a number of actual experiences, rooted in time and place.

But each point of departure is only that – a point of departure. For then the poem tends to general significance, but a significance that does not (or should not) lose touch with its concrete origin. Though not all of the following titles are in the present selection, they serve for illustration. The ten lines of "Panorama" evoke for the reader no more than the rooftops of a town viewed from a tower. It was not necessary to add in the title, "tower of the cathedral of Murcia"; but without Murcia, that poem would not have been born. "Everyone's Hope" is about a town's festival which centers around a symbol of hope. Its prototype was Good Friday morning in Seville, when the procession of the Virgin of Hope returns to its church in Triana. In "Death, from a Distance" – as Professor E. M. Wilson of Cambridge University was surprised to learn – "where the light of country fields is caught in the blind, final precinct of the dead, a wall takes aim" is not an abstraction. The author had in mind the white walls of the cemetery of Valladolid.

Certain other poems are not generalized beyond their particular points of departure. "Along Illustrious Shores" is a sketch of the bookstalls on the banks of the Seine in Paris. "Man's-Eye View" takes up another city panorama – this time at night – and is obviously a big city in the United States. (That "man" has New York in view.) In "Free Time," the longest poem in *Cántico* and the one which describes in the smallest detail a piece of Nature, we find ourselves on the campus of Wellesley College, standing beside a pond.... And so, through years of upheaval and despite many vicissitudes, this poetry of affirmation continued toward its fulfillment. Affirmation

6

of being, of reality, of life; affirmation which nonetheless recognized the forces of hostility.

But after *Cántico* there had to come a work in which the negative elements – evil, disorder and death – were developed. And so *Clamor* followed. Its first part, *Maremágnum* (Pandemonium), appeared in 1957 and the second, ... *Que van a dar en la mar,* in 1960. All Spanish readers will recognize in the latter title an allusion to the lines of Jorge Manrique, *"Nuestras vidas son los rios que van a dar en la mar, que es el morir"* – "our lives are the rivers that flow down to the sea, which is death." The third part of *Clamor,* which was published last year, is called *A la altura de las circunstancias.* This title comes from Antonio Machado's words, *"Es más difícil estar a la altura de las circunstancias que au-dessus de la mêlée"* – "it is more difficult to rise to the occasion than to stand above the conflict."

Clamor is concerned with new reaches of the poetic register: satire, elegy, and moral and narrative poems. Meanwhile, a third work is in progress. *Homenaje* (Homage) will be a verse miscellany of homages to writers and friends, poems based on reading, occasional poems, translations, etc. (an "etc." of great latitude: of world, man, love). May there be time to bring these three works together in a single volume, so that, for better or worse, that dream of my youth may be attained: to write a book, *one* book.

III

What is *Cántico*, this dialogue between man and the world, trying to say? Man knows himself only through his contact with a beyond; he sees himself inescapably caught up in something that infinitely surpasses him. Hence his wonderment. Above all, *Cántico* is a song in praise of the oneness of all being. Whoever experiences this oneness can never feel isolated. One must cherish and advance this privilege of being among all things that have being, of sharing in their fullness. Man affirms himself in affirming Creation; he shares in a universal value, though his part will always be the lesser.

This basic intuition is not restricted to persons who are endowed with a special sensitivity. There is no mysticism here; no experience is more ordinary. It is so ordinary, in fact, that we tend to be oblivious of it and pass our days without giving thought to this foundation on which we rest. Only when it is interrupted do we notice the *balance* in our everyday lives and our everyday surroundings. Otherwise, it is as if nothing were happening. Nothing? Only the array of forces that join together with incredible certainty. Up to a point, the human animal succeeds in fitting into his environment, and this adjustment between his eyes and the light of day, between his lungs and the air, between his feet and the ground involves a coordination so obvious that even the most observant persons are barely aware of it. This harmony does not clamor for man's attention. Yet no harmony is greater than our familiar equilibrium. *Cántico* is about these moments in which nothing occurs but the extraordinary phenomenon of normality.

On such occasions a joy both physical and metaphysical bursts forth, becoming the basis of an enthusiastic conviction, a faith: faith in reality, in the reality of this earth. The things of this world reveal themselves as objects, dense with their own being, in accord with their definition, true to their essence. It is not the beauty of these realities that matters but their abundance, for they exist even in the humblest particle of our planet. But they are exactly what they are. This is the point.

Such a view calls for an awareness of the presence, the immediacy, of things in space and the present moment in time. This awareness carries with it the much-desired revelation, and the beyond is converted into an immediate and irrefutable end. In the present moment of time one looks not for conflict but for connection and maximum generosity. Past and future lie latent as ideas. Only the present is real, although the unreflecting person is not conscious of its palpitation and regards as without time any act taking place *now*. All roads lead one to the universe at its pinnacle of abundance, of consistency, of health.

The human animal wants to become man, man within his community. This applies, above all, to youth. (There are no old people in *Cántico*.) Friendship emerges as the high point of living together. The whole of *Cántico* is an ascension toward love. And not because love is the force that moves the sun and other stars. Thanks to love we attain the fullness of reality, and experience in its closest linking the oneness of body and soul. By love "the here and now" is compelled to yield its greatest treasure. The act of love – a song of songs born always anew – surges and resurges. Love as creation; and foremost the lovers themselves, always real. Paradise knows neither nostalgia for the past nor longing for the future. *Cántico* presents reality as it is. No candle is more real than the actual candle, the one that burns. For now, at least, we have our presence on this earth before us.

Cántico assumes a relatively balanced relation between a sane and free protagonist and a world in plumb. But this relationship exists within a field of conflicting forces. The luminous center, on which our attention converges, is besieged. Disaster and disorder, affliction and evil, time and death – all do their damage and upset the balance, wrecking the symmetry. When men nullify the chaos, there is a world; but such moments are not always attained, for everything is subject to compromise within the conflicts of History. In disorder, evil is always at work, and therefore the world's vision must be ethical. This is the faith that sustains *Cántico*: evil does not prevail.

Affliction, too, shows its sinister face, always standing in opposition to the most determined resistance. Affliction weakens or destroys the unity of being. Of course, affliction also forms and shapes, ennobles and strengthens; without it there is no life. But the truly normal man never abandons himself to affliction. The consistency of *Cántico* does not allow such conduct. Fortunate and unfortunate incidents are constantly taking place throughout time. Temporality is mortality. Death is no more than the last dictate of life itself. Realizing that death will not rise up on the horizon to give life its bearings, we ought to resign ourselves to meeting death with serenity. To live is not to go dying; mortality is not death.

All these destructive and negative influences make up the chorus of *Cántico*, a chorus of minor voices, subordinate to the singing voice. Their existence within the whole suffices. Only in this way, avoiding suppressions and distortions that would alter the truth, can the whole be really whole. Affirmation of reality rises above the medley of bitterness, for man never gives in to cowardly resignation. But positive and negative values are not dissociated; they meet in this unifying vision. *Cántico* emphasizes an attachment to reality as it is. In these poems we look at ourselves – as we *must* look at ourselves – face to face. Man does not submit to his enemies without a contest. *Cántico* erects a bulwark for the effort of being, for the struggle against non-being. The gift of life is not taken for granted; above all, one exercises the will to live. *Cántico* . . . a song, then, in praise of contemplation and action, both directed toward one end alone – to bring to life an awareness of the wholeness of being on this earth. What happens in *Cántico*? Nothing more than the huge converging of Creation.

Anyone contemplating this convergence could sum up

his amazement in very few words: "It's a well-made world." The world as a glory of Creation, which understands its shortcomings and its excellence. Yet nothing is truer than that "this world of man is badly made." Not that other world, however, which is superior to man. Never in *Cántico* are Society and Creation confused; there is not a single line concerning the accumulated past or present of History. *Cántico* is an act of attentiveness. Despite many obstacles it tends toward serenity, toward joy – with wonder and with gratitude. Experience of being, affirmation of life, of this life on earth which has a value in itself and now – *cántico*, a song of praise.

CÁNTICO
In Praise of Living

Tregastel, Brittany
1919-1950
Wellesley, Massachusetts

I

IN THE WAKE OF YOUR WINGS

Return, dove, return,
That the wounded deer
May appear on the hillside
In the wake of your wings
And breathe new freshness.

SAN JUAN DE LA CRUZ

MÁS ALLÁ

I

(El alma vuelve al cuerpo,
Se dirige a los ojos
Y choca.) —¡Luz! Me invade
Todo mi ser. ¡Asombro!

Intacto aún, enorme,
Rodea el tiempo ... Ruidos
Irrumpen. ¡Cómo saltan
Sobre los amarillos

Todavía no agudos
De un sol hecho ternura
De rayo alboreado
Para estancia difusa,

Mientras van presentándose
Todas las consistencias
Que al disponerse en cosas
Me limitan, me centran!

¿Hubo un caos? Muy lejos
De su origen, me brinda
Por entre hervor de luz
Frescura en chispas. ¡Día!

BEYOND

I

(Spirit turns back to the body,
Moves toward the eyes,
And strikes home.) All my being
Flows in on me. Daylight, O thunderstruck!

Still intact and tremendous,
Time sweeps its great circle. The clangor
Of voices assaults us. How they leap
On the yellows —

Not vehement yet —
Of a sunlight gone tender,
A glitter already made morning's,
Suffusing an interval,

While the sensible bulk of the world
Proffers its substance, composes
Itself in the matrix of things
That bounds and concenters me.

Was there a Chaos? Remote
From its origin, through the ferment
Of brightness, fresh scintillations
Salute me. Morning!

Una seguridad
Se extiende, cunde, manda.
El esplendor aploma
La insinuada mañana.

Y la mañana pesa,
Vibra sobre mis ojos,
Que volverán a ver
Lo extraordinario: todo.

Todo está concentrado
Por siglos de raíz
Dentro de este minuto,
Eterno y para mí.

Y sobre los instantes
Que pasan de continuo
Voy salvando el presente,
Eternidad en vilo.

Corre la sangre, corre
Con fatal avidez.
A ciegas acumulo
Destino: quiero ser.

Ser, nada más. Y basta.
Es la absoluta dicha.
¡Con la esencia en silencio
Tanto se identifica!

A certitude,
Commanding, augmenting itself,
Expanding a splendor that measures the reaches
Of imminent daylight,

As day presses heavily,
Flutters its pulse on my eyes
That open again and encounter
The visible marvel: everything.

All things, the millennial
Sum of our being, packed
Into the web of a minute
Eternally here, and my own.

As over the instant
That ranges in ceaseless succession
I pass through eternity's tension
To salvage the present.

The blood races on; it flows
With a fatal avidity.
A destiny blindly assembles
Itself: I *will* that I be.

To be – only that! It suffices
For pure delectation!
Thus, in a kinship of silence
To be one with the essences!

¡Al azar de las suertes
Únicas de un tropel
Surgir entre los siglos,
Alzarse con el ser,

Y a la fuerza fundirse
Con la sonoridad
Más tenaz: sí, sí, sí,
La palabra del mar!

Todo me comunica,
Vencedor, hecho mundo,
Su brío para ser
De veras real, en triunfo.

Soy, más, estoy. Respiro.
Lo profundo es el aire.
La realidad me inventa,
Soy su leyenda. ¡Salve!

II

No, no sueño. Vigor
De creación concluye
Su paraíso aquí:
Penumbra de costumbre.

Y este ser implacable
Que se me impone ahora
De nuevo —vaguedad
Resolviéndose en forma

In the risks of original
Hazard and the press of the world
To course amidst centuries,
Erect in my being!

To plant myself firmly
In the stress of unflinching
Sonority. Assuredly that!
Yes! Yes! The speech of the sea!

Conqueror, at one with the world,
To whom all things acknowledge,
Exulting, their rage for existence – to be
In reality real.

I am; I go on existing. I breathe.
Profundities move through the air.
I am reality's legend,
Contrived in reality. Hail!

II

No dream! All the might
Of creation composes
Its paradise here:
In the shadowy ring of the usual.

This implacable coming-to-be
That grapples me here
And renews itself – still indeterminate,
Resolving itself in the play

De variación de almohada,
En blancura de lienzo,
En mano sobre embozo,
En el tendido cuerpo

Que aun recuerda los astros
Y gravita bien— este
Ser, avasallador
Universal, mantiene

También su plenitud
En lo desconocido:
Un más allá de veras
Misterioso, realísimo.

III

¡Más allá! Cerca a veces,
Muy cerca, familiar,
Alude a unos enigmas.
Corteses, ahí están.

Irreductibles, pero
Largos, anchos, profundos
Enigmas —en sus masas.
Yo los toco, los uso.

Hacia mi compañía
La habitación converge.
¡Qué de objetos! Nombrados,
Se allanan a la mente.

Of mutations: in forms on my pillow,
In the whiteness of linen,
A hand on the counterpane's fold,
In the body outstretched –

Yet has all the stars in its memory
And rests on the balances –
The genius commanding
Creation, preserving

Its plenitude always
In the nameless and still to be known:
The truths beyond truth that elude
Us, arcane in the pith of the real.

III

Always beyond us! Yet close to us,
Very close to us, sometimes, familiar,
Invoking enigmas,
Intending some kindness. They are here.

Irreducible,
Expansive and spacy, enigmas
Remote in the concourse of masses.
I touch them, I use them;

Conclaves that move within range
Of my being, and converge.
All that volley of objects! Named by
     their names
They would ravage the knower.

Enigmas son y aquí
Viven para mi ayuda,
Amables a través
De cuanto me circunda

Sin cesar con la móvil
Trabazón de unos vínculos
Que a cada instante acaban
De cerrar su equilibrio.

IV

El balcón, los cristales,
Unos libros, la mesa.
¿Nada más esto? Sí,
Maravillas concretas.

Material jubiloso
Convierte en superficie
Manifiesta a sus átomos
Tristes, siempre invisibles.

Y por un filo escueto,
O al amor de una curva
De asa, la energía
De plenitud actúa.

¡Energía o su gloria!
En mi dominio luce
Sin escándalo dentro
De lo tan real, hoy lunes.

For their name is enigma; they stay
With us now for our good,
Beneficent still through the rout
Of whatever encircles us.

Unceasingly, link over link,
They join in that mobile concurrence,
Each moment unbolting its balances
And closing its changes anew.

IV

A balcony, window glass,
Some books, and a table.
Nothing more? Nothing more than that: only
These tangible prodigies.

These things, in a jubilee,
The sadness of atoms transfigured
In manifest surfaces,
Forever invisible.

Loosed by the edge of a blade,
Or curved to a haft that it
Fits to its love, the power
Within plenitude kindles.

Power, or the glories of power!
Here in my sovereignty, undefiled
In the mesh of the actual,
Today blazes: Monday.

Y ágil, humildemente,
La materia apercibe
Gracia de Aparición:
Esto es cal, esto es mimbre.

V

Por aquella pared,
Bajo un sol que derrama,
Dora y sombrea claros
Caldeados, la calma

Soleada varía.
Sonreído va el sol
Por la pared. ¡Gozosa
Materia en relación!

Y mientras, lo más alto
De un árbol —hoja a hoja
Soleándose, dándose,
Todo actual— me enamora.

Errante en el verdor
Un aroma presiento,
Que me regalará
Su calidad: lo ajeno,

Lo tan ajeno que es
Allá en sí mismo. ¡Dádiva
De un mundo irremplazable:
Voy por él a mi alma!

As nimbly and humbly,
The kingdom of matter divines
All the grace of Appearance: this
Is the quicklime, this the withe in the wicker.

V

Now on the plane of the wall,
In a sunlight that ripples
Its simmering clarities, gilding
And darkening the brim, the sunny

Tranquillity changes.
The smile of the sun passes over,
Traversing the wall – matter elate
In its perfect relations!

While the topmost ascents
Of a tree – leaf after leaf
Aloft in the sunlight, giving itself
To the sun – everything actual – delights me.

Vagrant in green,
A perfume discloses itself
That will hazard at length the reward
Of its properties: the distant –

The exceedingly distant, that lives on
In its single identity there. O gift
Of that never replaceable world:
I journey through you to my soul!

VI

¡Oh perfección: dependo
Del total más allá,
Dependo de las cosas!
¡Sin mí son y ya están

Proponiendo un volumen
Que ni soñó la mano,
Feliz de resolver
Una sorpresa en acto!

¡Dependo en alegría
De un cristal de balcón,
De ese lustre que ofrece
Lo ansiado a su raptor,

Y es de veras atmósfera
Diáfana de mañana,
Un alero, tejados,
Nubes allí, distancias!

Suena a orilla de abril
El gorjeo esparcido
Por entre los follajes
Frágiles. (Hay rocío.)

Pero el día al fin logra
Rotundidad humana
De edificio y refiere
Su fuerza a mi morada.

O Perfectness! All that surpasses me,
Lying beyond me, sustains me:
I depend on the things of this world!
On all that has being, that lives,

And that is not myself; that goes on
    propounding
A volume undreamt of by hands,
Intent on the bliss of an unforeseen
Wonder, resolved in an act!

I glean my delight
From the glass of a balcony window,
In the luster that tenders
A dream to its taker;

That is truly a part of the air
And the morning's transparency,
The shape of a gable, a vista of rooftops,
Clouds close to us, distances!

Among delicate foliage
(See – there is dew!) a warbling
Grows festive: it resounds
On the margins of April.

But daylight shall build from its fabric
A human rotundity,
And resign all its ardors at last
To the house of my wayfaring.

Así va concertando,
Trayendo lejanías,
Que al balcón por países
De tránsito deslizan.

Nunca separa el cielo.
Ese cielo de ahora
—Aire que yo respiro—
De planeta me colma.

¿Dónde extraviarse, dónde?
Mi centro es este punto:
Cualquiera. ¡Tan plenario
Siempre me aguarda el mundo!

Una tranquilidad
De afirmación constante
Guía a todos los seres,
Que entre tantos enlaces

Universales, presos
En la jornada eterna,
Bajo el sol quieren ser
Y a su querer se entregan

Fatalmente, dichosos
Con la tierra y el mar
De alzarse a lo infinito:
Un rayo de sol más.

Therefore, the crowding successions
That bear up the distances
And define from the balcony's verge
All that traffic of countries.

The sky will not rend itself.
The immediate sky —
The air that I breathe —
Makes me brim to the planets.

How go wide of the mark? How
Founder? This point is my center:
Wheresoever I choose it. Forever prodigious,
The sheltering keep of the world!

A consented tranquillity
Changelessly shows us the way:
All things that have being,
At large in the clasp

And the weave of the universe,
Captive in daylight's eternity,
All beings under the sun that burn
For their being, and contrive from their wish

Fatally, luckily,
Out of rubble and sea water,
To heave themselves into the infinite:
Another scintilla of sun.

Es la luz del primer
Vergel, y aun fulge aquí,
Ante mi faz, sobre esa
Flor, en ese jardín.

Y con empuje henchido
De afluencias amantes
Se ahinca en el sagrado
Presente perdurable

Toda la creación,
Que al despertarse un hombre
Lanza la soledad
A un tumulto de acordes.

Toward that original pleasance, alight,
Still shedding its lusters,
Showing itself to my eyes, touching
The shape of that flower, there in that
    garden –

While, in the thrust and the drench
Of adoring affinities,
The whole of creation
Plants itself into the perduring

Present, this immediate blessedness,
That sends all its solitude forth
Through a tumult of concord,
To startle the sleep of a man.

BEN BELITT

LOS NOMBRES

Albor. El horizonte
Entreabre sus pestañas
Y empieza a ver. ¿Qué? Nombres.
Están sobre la pátina

De las cosas. La rosa
Se llama todavía
Hoy rosa, y la memoria
De su tránsito, prisa,

Prisa de vivir más.
¡A largo amor nos alce
Esa pujanza agraz
Del Instante, tan ágil

Que en llegando a su meta
Corre a imponer Después!
¡Alerta, alerta, alerta,
Yo seré, yo seré!

¿Y las rosas? Pestañas
Cerradas: horizonte
Final. ¿Acaso nada?
Pero quedan los nombres.

NAMES

Dawn. The horizon
Unlocks its eyelashes
And begins to see. What? Names.
They hover over the film

Of things. The rose
Today is still called
Rose, and the memory
Of its passage, eager,

Eager for more life.
May the unfledged power
Of the Instant – so agile
That in reaching its goal

It leaps to build Another –
Lift us to a long love!
Look out! Look out! Look out!
I will be! I will be!

And the roses? Locked
Eyelashes: the last
Horizon. Possibly nothing?
But still the names remain.

STEPHEN BERG

NATURALEZA VIVA

¡Tablero de la mesa
Que, tan exactamente
Raso nivel, mantiene
Resuelto en una idea

Su plano: puro, sabio,
Mental para los ojos
Mentales! Un aplomo,
Mientras, requiere al tacto,

Que palpa y reconoce
Cómo el plano gravita
Con pesadumbre rica
De leña, tronco, bosque

De nogal. ¡El nogal
Confiado a sus nudos
Y vetas, a su mucho
Tiempo de potestad

Reconcentrada en este
Vigor inmóvil, hecho
Materia de tablero
Siempre, siempre silvestre!

NATURE ALIVE

The panel board of the table,
That smooth plane precisely
True to a hair, holds up
Its level form, sustained

By an idea: pure, exact,
The mind's image before
The mind's eyes! And yet,
Full assurance needs the touch

That explores and discovers
How the formal idea sags back
Down to the rich heaviness
Of kindling, trunk and timber

Of walnut. The walnut wood,
Secure in its own whorls
And grains, assured of its long
Season of so much strength

Now fused into the heart
Of this quiet vigor, the stuff
Of a table board, remains
Always, always wild!

JAMES WRIGHT

JARDÍN EN MEDIO

Para Emilio
claridad caliente y cincelada.
GABRIEL MIRÓ

Azoteas, torres, cúpulas
Aproximan los deseos
De las calles y las plazas
A su cielo.

Vacación.
¡Nubes, nubes de bureo!
Libres, lentas,
Varían, vagan sin término.

Luminoso el redondel,
La ciudad confusa dentro,
Mayo sin prisa por Junio
Se abandona a su entretiempo.

Buen desorden:
En el rumor un concierto
Se insinúa
Silencioso. ¡Dulce estrépito!

Cercada por el bullicio,
De seguro no está lejos
De nadie la realidad
De un portento.

THE GARDEN IN THE MIDDLE

For Emilio

warm and chiseled clarity.

GABRIEL MIRÓ

Flat roofs, towers, domes
Approximate the desires
Of the streets and squares
    For their heaven.

    Holiday.
Clouds, clouds of amusement!
    Slow, unattached, they
Shift, wander without a goal.

A luminous circle,
A city blurred from within,
May, unhastening toward June,
Abandons itself to its own interval.

    Wholesome disorder:
Into a murmur, harmony
    Winds itself
Silently. Pleasant noise!

Walled in by the uproar,
Surely no one is far away
From the reality
    Of a miracle.

¡Oh soleada clausura!
Recoleto
Queda todo frente al sol,
Bajo el viento.

Hora en limpio.
La fila de los abetos
Traza al fondo
Su horizonte verdinegro.

¿Un mirlo será quien pía?
El gorjeo
Surge de unas hojas tiernas
De revuelo.

Se preguntan, se responden
Ya dos fresnos.
Buches se adivinan fatuos,
Grosezuelos.

No faltan ni mariposas
Tendiendo sus aleteos
Al azar sobre las trémulas
Corolas de los reflejos.

Entre la luz y el olor
Pasa goloso el insecto
Con afán desordenado
Que se ahonda en embeleso.

O sunny isolation,
            Composure of spirit,
Everything keeps its face to the sun,
            Under the wind.

            Purifying hour.
The line of fir trees
            Traces to the very bottom
Its horizon of dark green.

For whom will a blackbird cry?
            The warbling
Surges out of the young leaves,
            Stirring.

And yet, two ash trees question
            And answer each other.
Even the necks of little birds appear foolish,
            Puffed up.

And there is a plenty of butterflies,
Extending the flutter of their wings,
Riskily, over the tremulous
Corollas of their reflections.

Between the light and the fragrance
A sweet-toothed insect passes
With bewildered eagerness,
That deepens into rapture.

Hasta margaritas hay
Distantes, allá en su reino,
Y algún botón amarillo,
Feliz de ser tan concreto.

Cabrillea un agua viva,
Rayo a rayo sonriendo.
La sombra sobre las márgenes
Se difunde como oreo.

¡Qué buen calor! Un ambiente
            De secreto,
Banco, follaje, penumbra,
            Sol inmenso.

¿Sobrará tanta belleza?
            Yo la quiero.
Basta acaso que un ocioso
            Goce, lento.

            Paraíso:
Jardín, una paz sin dueño,
            Y algún hombre
Con su minuto sereno.

Tanta comunicación
Sin descanso entre los juegos
Más remotos me regala
Mucho más de cuanto espero.

Even the daisies
Have a kingdom, off in the distance,
With some yellow bud or other,
Happy at being a solid form.

And a quick water combs out,
Glitter on glitter, smiling.
The shadow on the margins
Is scattered like fresh air.

What comely warmth! An environment
     In hiding,
Bench, foliage, penumbra,
     Immense sunlight.

Will so much beauty spill over?
     I want it to spill.
Maybe a slow, useless
     Joy is enough.

     Paradise:
Garden, peace without an owner,
     And some man
In his serene moment.

So much exchange of meaning,
Unresting between the extremes
Of motion, delights me further
Than many things that I look for.

¡Ancho espacio libre, césped,
Olmo a solas en el centro,
Con ahinco poseído
    Mi silencio!

Mas . . . ¿Otra vez? He ahí,
    Recompuesto,
El discorde mundo en torno,
    Tan ajeno.

    Por el aire
Flotan, de un rumor suspensos,
    Muchos cruces
De otras voces y otros genios.

Ventura, ventura mínima:
¿Quién te arrancará del hecho
Mismo de vivir? ¡Vivir
Aún y el morir tan cierto!

He ahí la realidad
Revuelta: fárrago acerbo.
¿Y el jardín? ¿Dónde un jardín?
    —En el medio.

Broad free space, lawn,
Elm alone in the center,
And my silence, mastered
            After a struggle!

But . . . another time? Look there,
            Gathered again,
The discordant world, turning,
            So alien.

            Through the air,
With a suspended murmur,
            Float many crossthreads
Of other voices and other presences.

Happiness, the smallest happiness:
Who will uproot you
From this fact of living? Living
Still, and dying so certain!

Here is reality,
Tangled: a raucous confusion.
And the garden? Where is there a garden?
            Right in the middle.

                    JAMES WRIGHT

DESCANSO EN JARDÍN

Los astros avanzan entre
    Nubarrones
Hacia el último jardín.
    Losas, flores.

¿Qué del incidente humano?
    Calma en bloque.
Los muertos están más muertos
    Cada noche.

Mármoles, frondas iguales:
    Verde el orden.
Sobre el ciprés unos astros:
    Más verdores.

Muriendo siguen los muertos.
    ¡Bien se esconden,
Entre la paz y el olvido,
    Sin sus nombres!

Haya para el gran cansancio
    Sombra acorde.
Los astros se acercan entre
    Nubarrones.

REPOSE OF GARDENS

The planets advance among
    Thunderheads
Toward the ultimate garden.
    Gravestones, flowers.

And what of the human occasion?
    A monolith's calm.
The dead are more dead
    As night follows night.

Marbles, identical fronds:
    Gradations of verdure.
Over the cypresses, planets:
    More green in its prime.

The dead go on with their dying.
    How well they conceal themselves
Between peace and oblivion,
    Shorn of their names!

On that massive repose
    May the darkness fall suitably!
The planets draw near among
    Thunderheads now.

BEN BELITT

47

¿Rosas? Pero el alba.
. . . Y el recién nacido.
(¡Qué guardada el alma!)
Follajes ya: píos.

Muelle carne vaga,
Sueño en su espesura,
Cerrazón de calma,
Espera difusa.

Rosas —para el alba.
Pura sí, no alegre,
Se esboza la gracia.
¡Oh trémulas fuentes!

Creaciones, masa,
Desnudez, hoyuelos.
La facción exacta
Relega lo eterno.

¿Ya apuntan cerradas
Aún, sí, sonrisas?
. . . La aurora (¿Y el alba?)
¡Oh rosas henchidas!

CRADLE, ROSES, BALCONY

Roses, then? Rather, the dawn.
. . . Whatever is newly born to the world.
(How watchful the spirit!)
Later with leafage: a twittering.

Supple and tentative flesh,
In its dreaming intensity
A thunderhead in the calm,
A wandering vigil.

Certainly, roses – as if for a dawn.
Immaculate surely, though somberly:
So the beauty disposes itself.
O tremulous fountains!

Creations, concretions,
A nakedness, dimpling.
A contour's exactitude
Annuls the eternal.

As still undisclosed, but
Nonetheless imminent there, the smiling
Emerges . . . The daybreak. (Or shall
    it be morning?)
Ah, surfeit of roses!

                              BEN BELITT

EL SEDIENTO

¡Desamparo tórrido!
La acera de sombra
Palpita con toros
Ocultos. Y topan.

Un sol sin aleros,
Masa de la tarde,
Convierte en silencio
De un furor el aire.

¡De prisa, que enfrente
La verja franquea
Su reserva! Huele,
Huele a madreselva.

Penumbra de olvido
Guardan las persianas.
Sueño con un frío
Que es amor, que es agua.

¡Ah! Reveladora,
El agua de un éxtasis
A mi sed arroja
La eternidad. —¡Bebe!

THE THIRSTER

Torrid desolation!
The shaded sidewalk
Shudders with hidden
Bulls. And they crash head on.

A sun without eaves,
Dough of the afternoon,
The sun changes from
A fury to silence.

Hurry, for before us
The grill has swung wide to offer
Its preserve! From within rise
Odors, odors of honeysuckle.

The window blinds retain
The penumbra of oblivion.
A dream together with a coldness
Which is love, which is water.

Ah, bringing revelation,
The water of an ecstasy
Upon my thirst slakes
Eternity. – Drink!

W. S. MERWIN

EL OTOÑO: ISLA

El otoño: isla
De perfil estricto,
Que pone en olvido
La onda indecisa.

¡Amor a la línea!
La vid se desnuda
De una vestidura
Demasiado rica.

Y una canastilla
De alegres racimos
Cela un equilibrio
De sueños en minas.

Estilo en la dicha,
Sapiencia en el pasmo,
Entre errante fausto
La rama sencilla.

¿Dulce algarabía?
Agudo el ramaje
Niega ya a las aves
Música escondida.

AUTUMN: ISLAND

Autumn: island
Of strict profile
That shoves the hesitant wave
Into oblivion.

A love of line!
The grapevine is stripped
Of a garment
Overly rich.

And a small basket
Of jubilant bunches
Conceals an equilibrium
Of potential dreams.

Style in the joy,
Wisdom in the wonder,
Among scattered pomp
The mere branch.

Sweet babbling?
The bare branches
Deny the birds
Their hidden concerts.

¡Oh claridad! Pía
Tanto entre las hojas
Que quieren ser todas
A un tiempo amarillas.

¡Trabazón de brisas
Entre cielo y álamo!
Y todo el espacio,
Tan continuo, vibra.

Esta luz antigua
De tarde feliz
No puede morir.
¡Ya es mía, ya es mía!

—Pronto, pronto, ensilla
Mi mejor caballo.
El camino es ancho
Para mi porfía.

O splendor! So much
Chirping in the leaves
That all want to be
Yellow at the same time.

The work of breezes
Joining sky and poplar!
And all space,
Endlessly, throbs.

This ancient light
Of a pleasant afternoon
Cannot die.
Now it's mine! Now it's mine!

– Hurry, hurry, saddle
My best horse.
The road widens
For my insistent will.

STEPHEN BERG

LO ESPERADO

Tras los flacos esquemas
Trémulos de las sombras
Que al dichoso en potencia
Por un atajo acosan,

Después de tantas noches
Arqueadas en túneles
De una luna entre roces
De silencio y de nube,

Aquí está lo esperado.
El doliente vacío
Va poblándose. ¡Pájaros!
Aquí mismo, aquí mismo,

Dentro de la absoluta
Sazón de una evidencia
Que obliga a la aventura
De quien por fin no sueña,

El alma, sin perder
El cuerpo, va creando
Su plenitud: nivel
Pasmoso de la mano.

THE HOPED-FOR

Across the frail tremulous
Symbols of the shadows
Which pursue, through a short cut,
The fortunate man in his power,

After so many nights
Arched over in tunnels
By a moon rubbed
Between silence and cloud,

Here is what was hoped for.
The aching emptiness
Grows populous. Birds!
Here, in this very place

Within the absolute
Season of an evidence
Which compels to his adventure
Him who at last is not dreaming,

The soul, without losing
The body, proceeds to create
Its plenitude: wonderful
Level of the hand.

W. S. MERWIN

SALVACIÓN DE LA PRIMAVERA

I

Ajustada a la sola
Desnudez de tu cuerpo,
Entre el aire y la luz
Eres puro elemento.

¡Eres! Y tan desnuda,
Tan continua, tan simple
Que el mundo vuelve a ser
Fábula irresistible.

En torno, forma a forma,
Los objetos diarios
Aparecen. Y son
Prodigios, y no mágicos.

Incorruptibles dichas,
Del sol indisolubles,
A través de un cristal
La evidencia difunde

Con todo el esplendor
Seguro en astro cierto.
Mira cómo esta hora
Marcha por esos cielos.

A SPRINGTIME SALVATION

I

At rest, in your body's
Singular nudity,
Between light and the air,
You are pure element.

And are, in that nakedness,
So continuous and simple
That the world again shows itself
Irresistible fable.

Around you, form after form,
Habitual objects
Display themselves to our sight – and are
Magic no longer, but prodigy.

Incorruptible joys,
Indissoluble gifts of the sun
That through a window glass
Scatters its evidence

With all the infallible
Pomp of a positive star.
See now how the hour
Moves through those heavens.

II

Mi atención, ampliada,
Columbra. Por tu carne
La atmósfera reúne
Términos. Hay paisaje.

Calmas en soledad
Que pide lejanía
Dulcemente a perderse
Muy lejos llegarían,

Ajenas a su propia
Ventura sin testigo,
Si ya tanto concierto
No convirtiese en íntimos

Esos blancos tan rubios
Que sobre su tersura
La mejor claridad
Primaveral sitúan.

Es tuyo el resplandor
De una tarde perpetua.
¡Qué cerrado equilibrio
Dorado, qué alameda!

II

My wakefulness, widening,
Glimpses some certainty. The atmosphere
Gathers all boundary
Into your flesh. All landscape is there.

Still, in a solitude
That asks for its distances
Shyly, and vanishes there,
All calms would outjourney themselves,

Unwitnessed or lost
To their own consummation,
If that pure coalescence of things
Did not bring in more intimate range

Both the blonde and the brilliant,
And apportion the sovereign
Transparence of spring
To illumine their purity.

Noon's splendor
Is timeless and yours:
What closes of gold equilibrium,
What green promenades!

III

Presa en tu exactitud,
Inmóvil regalándote,
A un poder te sometes,
Férvido, que me invade.

¡Amor! Ni tú ni yo,
Nosotros, y por él
Todas las maravillas
En que el ser llega a ser.

Se colma el apogeo
Máximo de la tierra.
Aquí está : la verdad
Se revela y nos crea.

¡Oh realidad, por fin
Real, en aparición!
¿Qué universo me nace
Sin velar a su dios?

Pesa, pesa en mis brazos,
Alma, fiel a un volumen.
Dobla con abandono,
Alma, tu pesadumbre.

III

Fixed in your certainty,
The unshakable gift of yourself,
You yield your self up to the powers
That inhabit me wholly.

O Love! Neither you nor myself –
But *we* – love's integer
Wise in all marvels
By which Being comes into its being.

Earth's fullness brims over,
The pitch of the possible;
It is here: truth makes itself known
To us, and contrives our existence.

O Reality, conclusive
And real to us now in presences!
What world gives me life
Without warding its godhead?

Bear down, bear down in my arms,
Shadow intent upon substance. O Soul,
Put off circumspection
And redouble your gravity.

IV

Y los ojos prometen
Mientras la boca aguarda.
Favorables, sonríen.
¡Cómo intima, callada!

Henos aquí. Tan próximos,
¡Qué oscura es nuestra voz!
La carne expresa más.
Somos nuestra expresión.

De una vez paraíso,
Con mi ansiedad completo,
La piel reveladora
Se tiende al embeleso.

¡Todo en un solo ardor
Se iguala! Simultáneos
Apremios me conducen
Por círculos de rapto.

Pero más, más ternura
Trae la caricia. Lentas,
Las manos se demoran,
Vuelven, también contemplan.

IV

The eyes offer pledges
While the mouth waits, expectant.
Propitious, they smile
With such intimate diffidence!

We are joined. O how darkly
Our voices resound in that nearness!
The flesh is more eloquent:
It utters the thing that we are.

Instantaneous Eden,
All yearning made perfect,
Flesh puts off its secrecy
And stretches itself in a transport.

All things, identically joined
In a single felicity. All stresses
Converging at once
Where beatitude wheels,

While our touches' endearments make
Tenderness great. It grows greater. Gravely
Our hands delay their caresses
And return them again, like a thought.

V

¡Sí, ternura! Vosotros,
Soberanos, dejadme
Participar del orden:
Dos gracias en contraste,

Valiendo, repartiéndose.
¿Sois la belleza o dos
Personales delicias?
¿Qué hacer, oh proporción?

Aunque ... Brusco y secreto,
Un encanto es un orbe.
Obsesión repentina
Se centra, se recoge.

Y un capricho celeste
Cándidamente luce,
Improvisa una gloria,
Se va. Le cercan nubes.

Nubes por variación
De azares se insinúan,
Son, no son, sin cesar
Aparentes y en busca.

Si de pronto me ahoga,
Te ciega un horizonte
Parcial, tan inmediato
Que se nubla y se esconde,

V

Tenderness, certainly! You sovereign
Presences, I would honor
The decorum of things:
Two graces, contrasting,

Contending, bestowing themselves.
Are you Beauty, intact in itself,
Or two blissful identities?
To what purpose, Proportion?

Nonetheless . . . Ruthless and secretive,
Enchantment contracts like a globe;
The wayward obsession
Collects and concenters itself,

The blessed vagary
That guilelessly lights
A provisional glory,
Departs from us. Clouds close us in.

Clouds, or disaster's
Mutations that enter by stealth,
And are, or are not again, displaying
Themselves ceaselessly, ceaselessly following.

Should it smother me there,
And the partial horizon
Darken your vision – however
It cloud or conceal itself,

La plenitud en punto
De la tan ofrecida
Naturaleza salva
Su comba de armonía.

¡Amar, amar, amar,
Ser más, ser más aún!
¡Amar en el amor,
Refulgir en la luz!

Una facilidad
De cielo nos escoge
Para lanzarnos hacia
Lo divino sin bordes.

Y acuden, se abalanzan
Clamando las respuestas.
¿Ya inminente el arrobo?
¡Durase la inminencia!

¡Afán, afán, afán
A favor de dulzura,
Dulzura que delira
Con delirio hacia furia,

Furia aun no, más afán,
Afán extraordinario,
Terrible, que sería
Feroz, atroz o . . .! Pasmo.

The total excess of the world —
The nature that offers itself
With such bounty — upholds
The harmonious vault of the curve.

To love, always to love! to love
And to multiply being — to be always more!
To love in love's plenitude,
In the center of brightness, to brighten!

Some simple expedience
Of heaven has chosen us, surely,
To hurl us forth bodily
To immutable providence,

While our jubilant answers
Reply in their kind and fling themselves
Outward. Is some glory at hand?
May its imminence cling to us!

Ardently, ardently, ardently!
Ardor that mediates sweetness,
Sweetness intent upon ecstasy,
Ecstasy dazzling like rage —

Beyond all satiety: more ardently still,
Ardor in overplus,
Ardor ferocious and terrible,
Intent on atrocity — then:

F

¿Lo infinito? No. Cesa
La angustia insostenible.
Perfecto es el amor:
Se extasía en sus límites.

¡Límites! Y la paz
Va apartando los cuerpos.
Dos yacen, dos. Y ceden,
Se inclinan a dos sueños.

¿Irá cruzando el alma
Por limbos sin estorbos?
Lejos no está. La sombra
Se serena en el rostro.

VI

El planeta invisible
Gira. Todo está en curva.
Oye ahora a la sangre.
Nos arrastra una altura.

Desde arriba, remotos,
Invulnerables, juntos,
A orillas de un silencio
Que es abajo murmullos,

Murmullos que en los fondos
Quedan bajo distancias
Unidas en acorde
Sumo de panorama,

The spasm. Infinitude? No.
The untenable frenzy subsides.
It fades on the quick of the passional
And love is made perfect.

On the limits of appetite. There
All flesh disengages itself. Two bodies
Lie there, in their peace. Two yield
   themselves up,
Two lean separately into their dream.

Does the soul, in that dream,
Go on crossing its limbos unhindered?
It stands near to us still: its shadow
Falls stresslessly on our faces.

VI

The invisible planet
Whirls. All things rise in a curve.
Hear how the apogee
Pulls at our blood!

There above us, remote
And invulnerable, intact
On the edge of that stillness
Underlying all utterance,

Even as utterance calls out
In the depths underlying all distance,
Stilled in the perfect
Repose of a landscape –

Vemos cómo se funden
Con el aire y se ciernen
Y ahondan, confundidos,
Lo eterno, lo presente.

A oscuras, en reserva
Por espesor y nudo,
Todo está siendo cifra
Posible, todo es justo.

VII

Nadie sueña y la estancia
No resurge habitual.
¡Cuidado! Todavía
Sigue aquí la verdad.

Para siempre en nosotros
Perfección de un instante,
Nos exige sin tregua
Verdad inacabable.

¿Yo querré, yo? Querrá
Mi vida. ¡Tanto impulso
Que corre a mi destino
Desemboca en tu mundo!

Necesito sentir
Que eres bajo mis labios,
En el gozo de hoy,
Mañana necesario.

Self-confounded, now merged
With the air and outsoaring all vision,
Now piercing all things to the pith,
We look on the timeless and temporal.

Yet darkling we see them. At rest
In the palpable bulk of the world, naked,
A possible integer computes itself
Everywhere. The justness is all.

VII

Nobody sleeps; the habit of living
Has not entered our houses again.
Move warily there! The truth
Still is true to its image.

Within us, unchangeably,
The touch of an instant's perfection
Urges us on, without quarter,
To ineffable verity.

Shall I reckon my love, then? Not I;
But my lifetime shall name what it cherishes!
The instinct that flows toward my destiny
And empties itself in your world!

Mine always to feel you there, always
Within range of my lips:
Today's satisfaction
Tomorrow made exigent —

Nuestro mañana apenas
Futuro y siempre incógnito:
Un calor de misterio
Resguardado en tesoro.

VIII

Inexpugnable así
Dentro de la esperanza,
Sintiéndote alentar
En mi voz si me canta,

Me centro y me realizo
Tanto a fuerza de dicha
Que ella y yo por fin somos
Una misma energía,

La precipitación
Del ímpetu en su acto
Pleno, ya nada más
Tránsito enamorado,

Un ver hondo a través
De la fe y un latir
A ciegas y un velar
Fatalmente —por ti—

Para que en ese júbilo
De suprema altitud,
Allí donde no hay muerte,
Seas la vida tú.

Tomorrow that hardly divines
Its futurity, unknown to us always:
The glow of the mystery,
That treasure laid up for us there.

VIII

Unassailably fixed
In expectancy's center,
Hearing you breathe, if I sing,
In the breath of my singing,

I contract all my powers, and contrive
My reality joyfully: two
Identities – hers and my own – that
Must kindle as one, in the end:

One impulse made flesh
In the stroke of a manifest
Action, a loved possibility
Now intent on its changes;

A glimpse at the depths
Beyond all credulity; a blind
Palpitation; the fated
Watch of your destiny

That prepares, on the furthermost
Flight of its jubilance, one finality:
There where mortality ends,
Whatever lives on, shall be you.

¡Tú, tú, tú, mi incesante
Primavera profunda,
Mi río de verdor
Agudo y aventura!

¡Tú, ventana a lo diáfano:
Desenlace de aurora,
Modelación del día:
Mediodía en su rosa,

Tranquilidad de lumbre:
Siesta del horizonte,
Lumbres en lucha y coro:
Poniente contra noche,

Constelación de campo,
Fabulosa, precisa,
Trémula hermosamente,
Universal y mía!

¡Tú más aún: tú como
Tú, sin palabras toda
Singular, desnudez
Única, tú, tú sola!

IX

You, you eternally: you,
Ineffable Spring of my life,
River of vehement green
And dream of all enterprise;

Window that looks on transparency:
You are dawn's consummation
And day's metamorphoses:
Meridian's rose,

A calmed conflagration:
A horizon at rest,
Splendors conjoined and contending:
Night locked with the West –

Constellation alight in a field,
Unerring and fabulous,
A tremulous cosmos
Revealed, exquisitely mine!

The sum of the possible: you
As yourself, beyond language, at last
Naked and singular, your selfhood
Alone in your selfhood, all precedent passed.

BEN BELITT

II

APPOINTED HOURS

Fearing nothing, man sets for his labors
Appointed hours.

FRAY LUIS DE LEÓN

PASO A LA AURORA

I

Hay más alba, más alba en tanta lluvia.
Unánime fragor de creación: diluvia.
¡Agua de inmensidad!

               Choca en el barro,
Derrumbamiento aún que ya inicia un galope,
El despilfarro
Celeste de algún Lope.
¡Oh generosas nubes del impuro!
Chapotea en lo oscuro,
Galopando con su caballería,
Un caos que se forma
Su guía.
¿Caos en agresión no pide norma?

Alba y lluvia se funden. Con informe,
Quizá penoso balbuceo
Tiende a ser claro el día.
Apura el creador. ¡Querrá que se conforme
Su mundo a su deseo!
Todo, sí, rumoroso y prometido,
Se riza de recreo,
Todo puede ser nido.
. . . No más diluvio. Llueve.

PASSAGE TO DAWN

I

Dawn, there is more dawn in so much rain.
Unanimous clamor of creation: deluge.
Water of immensity!

            In the mud there beats
Even now the downpour, even now beginning a gallop:
The divine
Extravagance of a Lope.
O generous clouds of the impure!
There splashes in the darkness,
Galloping with horsemen,
A chaos improvising
Its own guide.
Does belligerent chaos need no paradigm?

Dawn and rain mingle. With formless,
Perhaps painful, babbling
The day gropes toward clarity.
The creator purifies and shapes
The world of his desire!
All, all, rustling and betrothed,
Rippling with delight,
Merges into nest:
. . . Deluge no longer. It is raining.

El agua determina con placer su goteo
Límpido y breve.
A través de un aire más libre la luz se atreve.

Término en desnudez, y sorprendida: tierra.
Con el frescor se esparce
La novedad intacta de un origen,
Que todavía yerra
Por entre los murmullos de su propio destino.
Con tal lluvia en las hojas aquel arce
Siente mejor los cielos que le rigen,
Y presiente quizá de dónde vino
—Tan nocturno el subsuelo y tan remoto—
Aquella profusión de copa manifiesta.
El agua viva abraza.
No hay coto
Que se cierre al afán de más floresta,
Floresta alboreante con su traza
De casi perfección en su frescura
De recién prorrumpida criatura.

Este candor —aroma
De terrones mojados—
Conduce a una amplitud por donde asoma
La claridad, aún escalofrío
También.
Palpita apareciendo aquella loma,
Trémula con sus prados,
Con su más que rocío.

Gladly the water, limpid and brief,
Ends its dropping.
Across a freer air the light ventures.

Finality in nakedness and surprise: earth.
There dallies with the coolness
The intact novelty of an origin,
Which even now wanders
Among the murmurs of its own destiny.
With its rain in the leaves the maple tree
Senses more strongly the skies that rule it,
And perhaps foresenses the source –
So nocturnal, so remote the underearth –
Of the manifest profusion of a branching tree.
The living water embraces:
No boundary is there
That checks its desire for further groves,
For groves dawning in profile
Nearly perfect in their coolness
Of the newly emerged creature.

This purity – the odor
Of wet clods –
Leads to a fullness where clarity,
Still shivering, also
Emerges.
That hillock trembles as it appears,
Quivers with its meadows,
With its surpassing dew.

Madrugador, un tren
—Y violento— zumba por entre el caserío
De los aún callados.
Hasta lejos del río
Temblor hay de ribera.
Todo en su luz naciente se aligera.

Y prorrumpe de nuevo el gran enlace.
Cándidas, inmediatas, confiadas,
Aguardan las posadas
En que el sol goza y yace.
Convertido en promesa,
El albor se enamora,
Y de querer no cesa
Con ímpetu de aurora.
¿Un instante del iris? Luz ilesa.
¡Qué terroso el olor, qué humedad tan humana!
He aquí, fiel prodigio, la mañana.

II

¿Vuelve todo a surgir como en primera vez,
Este universo es primitivo?
Mejor: todo resurge en esbeltez
Para ser más ... Aquel despliegue de ramaje
Con el retorcimiento varonil de un olivo,
El anónimo pájaro que avanza,
Mudo, sobre la hierba.
La esperanza está aquí. ¡Otra vez la esperanza

A train, early riser,
Buzzes – violent – among the clustered houses
Of those who are still quiet.
Even far from the river
There is a tremor of shore.
All becomes weightless in the rising light.

And the great commingling bursts forth anew.
Pure, immediate, serene
Await the dwellings
Where the sun basks and stretches.
Changed into promise
The whiteness plays a lover,
And will not cease from loving
With dawn's impulsiveness.
An instant of rainbow? Gentle light.
How earthy the smell, what human dampness!
And here, faithful prodigy, the morning.

II

Does all surge forth again as though for the first time?
Is this universe primitive?
Better: all surges again into elegance
For something more ... That unfurling of foliage
With the virile writhing of an olive tree,
That nameless bird who advances,
Mute, over the grass.
Hope is here. Hope once again

Tras el desvelo sin paisaje
—O soñado quizá—de noche acerba!
Aquí, sobre la cima
Ya clara,
Estar es renacer.
Hasta en lo más oculto, bajo tierra, se anima
Su tentación —latente— de algazara:
A plena luz la calidad de ser.

Fluye la luz en ondas amarillas,
Y sobre el horizonte golfos, lagos
Entregan sus orillas
A una trasformación en más capricho.
¡Oriente —sin tapices ni varillas
De magos!
Todo es nuevo... Tan nuevo que nadie aún lo ha dicho.
¡El sol! Y no deslumbra. Se remonta con lenta
Suavidad. ¡Ah, ninguno de existir se arrepienta!
Llegarán a su forma los materiales vagos.

¡El sol! Sobre las tierras, sobre las aguas, sobre
Los aires, ese fuego. Todo se le confía,
Nada quiere ser pobre.
¿Rosa, coral? Es realidad, es día.
Nadie columbra entonces —¡nubes!— la lejanía
Sin sentir otra vez que el suelo de la calle
No deja de ser valle,
A pesar de los hombres inminente.
Aquí están su posible silencio más sencillo,

After the vigil bereft of landscape –
Or vigil perhaps dreamed – of bitter night.
Here, on the summit
Already bright,
To be is to be reborn.
Even in the sunken and most hidden ground,
Though latent, there stirs the temptation to cry out:
Into full light the qualityof being.

The light flows in yellow waves.
And upon the horizon, gulfs, lakes
Give up their shores
To a transformation into further caprice.
Orient! Without the carpets or the wands
Of Magi.
All is new . . . So new that no one has spoken it.
The sun! And does not dazzle. Remounts with slow
Suavity. Ah, none repent of existing!
The vague materials shall attain their form.

The sun! Above the lands, above the waters, above
The airs, that fire. All surrenders to it;
Nothing wishes to be poor.
Rose? Coral? It is reality, it is day.
Then no one discerns – clouds! – the distance
Without again feeling that the pavement
Does not cease to be a valley
Imminent in spite of man.
Here is its possible more simple silence,

La misma primavera
Con aquella primera
Gran ventura sin gente,
Aquí están su follaje, su pájaro, su grillo.
Todo se suma necesariamente:
La pared soleada y mi consuelo,
Ese cristal y el cielo.

Un cristal de ventana
Se me ofrece y sujeta
La calle a la alegría de su diafanidad.
¡Oh ciudad bajo el sol, ciudad
Del sol, repleta
De gana!

¿La luz no es quien lo puso
Todo en su tentativa de armonía?
Este suelo de valle revelado es alfombra.
A los balcones sube, por la ciudad difuso,
Un runrún que va siendo rumor de compañía.
Extremo pacto:
El sol va a iluminar hasta la sombra.
Chispas hay con rocío que permanece intacto.
Todo, por fin, se nombra.

Suprema perfección: ese andar de muchacha,
Aurora en acto,
Facilidad, felicidad sin tacha.

Here the spring itself
With that first
Great unpeopled happiness,
Here are its foliage, its bird, its cricket.
All is heaped up, out of necessity:
My comfort and the sunny wall,
That glass, and the sky.

A windowpane
Offers itself to me, subjects
The street to the joy of its translucency.
O city under the sun, city
Of the sun, replete
With desire!

Is it not the light that places all
In its experiment in harmony?
This valley floor, revealed, is a carpet.
To the balconies, diffused through the city,
Rises a hum that is a rumor of crowds.
Extreme pact:
The sun is to illumine even the shadow.
There are sparks with a dew that stays intact.
All finds, at last, a name.

Supreme perfection: that gait of a girl,
Dawn in the act,
Facility, unstained felicity.

W. S. MERWIN

PRIMAVERA DELGADA

Cuando el espacio sin perfil resume
    Con una nube
Su vasta indecisión a la deriva,
    —¿Dónde la orilla?—
Mientras el río con el rumbo en curva
    Se perpetúa
Buscando sesgo a sesgo, dibujante,
    Su desenlace,
Mientras el agua duramente verde
    Niega sus peces
Bajo el profundo equívoco reflejo
    De un aire trémulo . . .
Cuando conduce la mañana, lentas,
    Sus alamedas
Gracias a las estelas vibradoras
    Entre las frondas,
A favor del avance sinuoso
    Que pone en coro
La ondulación suavísima del cielo
    Sobre su viento
Con el curso tan ágil de las pompas,
    Que agudas bogan . . .
¡Primavera delgada entre los remos
    De los barqueros!

DELICATE SPRING

When space without an outline ends up
    In cloud,
All that vast vagueness drifting downstream –
    Where is the bank? –
And while the river in its curving course
    Flows on and on
Searching slope after slope, as the designer
    Of its own undoing,
And while the water, of so dense a green,
    Conceals its very fish
Below the deep ambiguous reflection
    Of tremulous air . . .
When morning leads forth in stately file
    Its poplar avenues
Thanks to the watery wake shimmering there
    Between the leaves,
Furthering its winding progress
    That joins together,
Beneath its breeze, the sky's
    Gentlest undulation
With bubbles in their agile course
    Rowing so briskly on . . .
Between the oars of the boatmen,
    Delicate spring!

BARBARA HOWES

ESPERANZA DE TODOS

¡Esperanza de todos!
Y todos con el sol y la mañana
Se juntan en rumor,
En brillo sonreído,
En un aplauso que se va esparciendo
De la gente a la nube,
Del balcón a la espuma que se irisa
Junto al remo en realce
Festivo.
El barullo solar
Remueve de continuo los errantes
Pies que se arrastran con sus transeúntes
En búsqueda y espera.
¿Por dónde la esperanza?
Se aúpan a los árboles los niños,
Crecen entre las hojas.
Se perfilan en júbilo las verjas,
Ya del adolescente.
Un calor inicial, calor temprano
De la más compartida primavera,
Anuncia
La magnitud dichosa del estío.
Sobre el rumor difuso el grito pasa

EVERYONE'S HOPE

Everyone's hope!
And everyone with the sun and the morning
Gathered into a murmur,
Into a lustrous smile,
Into a praise that moves, delighting itself,
From the people to the cloud,
From the balcony to the iridescent foam,
Fused with the oar in a polish
Of festival.
The confusion of the sun
Continually stirs ambling feet
That crawl after the passers-by
In expectation and hope.
Where is this hope?
Boys help one another into the trees
And grow there, among the leaves.
Gratings, joyous in profile,
Hold the adolescents.
A beginning warmth, an early warmth
Of a spring wholly shared,
Announces
The lucky vastness of the summer.
On the widespread murmur, the cry passes

Lejos ya y disolviéndose,
Blando grito de nadie para nadie.
Llega a flotar un gozo que suaviza,
Si no impide, la discordancia al raso.
¡Batahola de fiesta,
De calor que es amigo,
De gente como bosque,
Bajo el sol multitud centelleante
De sonrisa y mirada,
Tan múltiples que pierden todo rumbo
Por entre tantos cruces
De rayo, savia y multitud que espera!
Esperanza: la esperanza de todos.
Un compás, un desfile,
Invocación, exclamación, loores,
—O nada más requiebros—
Y el río verde que desfila casi
Rojizo, si no sepia,
El río que acompaña
También,
De puente en puente primavera abajo,
Magno río civil de las historias.
¿Por dónde la esperanza?
La multitud se apiña hacia el relumbre,
Todo se estorba en una pleamar
Que se recibe como seña y dádiva
Del estío futuro.
¡Confusión —con un rayo
De sol buído sobre los metales,

To the distance, dissolving,
Bland cry of no one for no one.
If nothing impedes it, joy comes, floating,
Smoothing the discords into the open air.
The uproar of fiesta,
Of warmth that is a friend,
Of crowds like groves,
Under the sun the multitude flashing
With smiles and looks,
So many that they lose their way
Among so many crossroads
Of light, sap, and the searching multitude.
Hope: everyone's hope!
A compass, a parade,
Invocation, exclamation, praises –
Nothing more worthy of compliment –
And the green river that passes, nearly
Reddish, if not rich brown,
The river that encloses,
Likewise,
From bridge to bridge under the spring,
The great civil stream of history.
Where is hope?
The multitude crowds toward the brightness,
Hindering one another, to a flood tide
That they greet like a sign, a gift
Of summer to come.
Confusion – a ray
Of sharp-pointed sun on the metals,

Arneses, lentejuelas, terciopelos
De triunfo!
La esperanza valiente
Se interna, se difunde,
Hermosa, general:
Pueblo, compacto pueblo en ejercicio
De salud compartida,
De una salud como festivo don,
Como un lujo que allí se regalase.
Y sobre las aceras,
Algún lento celaje transeúnte.
Y las torres, las torres ataviadas
De simple abril en cierne,
Las torres desde siglos
—Ya sin orgullo— bellas para todos.
¿Por dónde al fin, por dónde?
Todos van juntos a esperar ahora,
Festivos,
A esperar la esperanza.
¡Oh virgen esperanza, si divina,
Tan abrazada al aire,
Y a la voz que más alto se remonta,
Y al silencio de muchos un momento!
Son muchos
A través de un rumor pacificado,
Muchos sobre su paz
De hombres,
En torno a su esperanza
De abril.

Harnesses, spangles, velvets
Of triumph!
The brave hope
Thrusts inward, scatters,
Beautiful, general:
A people, a gathered people, exercising
A health that is shared,
A health like a festive gift,
Like a luxury that delivers itself.
And upon the sidewalks,
Colorful clouds move past.
And the towers, the towers hung
With plain April in blossom,
The towers after centuries –
Without pride – beautiful for everyone.
Where, finally, where?
They gather to search now,
Festive,
To search for hope.
O virgin hope, so divine,
So embraced by the air,
And by the voice that towers over itself
And by the silence of many moments.
There are many,
In spite of a pacified rumor,
Many above the peace
Of men,
Turning back to their hope
Of April.

Y la sangre circula por los cuerpos,
Eficaz sin deber de sacrificio,
Sangre por esta espera.
¡Qué profunda la hora y matutina,
Feliz engalanada
Con su simple verdad primaveral!
Y se cruzan los vivas,
Altos vivas radiantes.
Bajo el azul, de súbito ... ¿Silencio?
Un vítor. ¡Vítor! La ovación en acto
De pura convergencia soleada.
¿Un coro? No. Mejor:
Abril común sobre una sola tierra,
¡Abril!
Es posible una vez
Enriquecerse en gozo por la suma
De tanto ajeno gozo,
Por la acumulación conmovedora
De claridad y espera.
En el aire un futuro
Libre, libre de muerte
—O con vida en la muerte, más allá.
¡Esperanza en la vida inacabable
Para mí, para todos,
Vía libre a las horas!
Grito hacia sol, raudal, nivel de fiesta.
La multitud se ahinca en su alegría,
Y todo se reúne,
Feraz.
¡Esperanza de todos!

And the blood flows through their bodies,
Efficient, owing no sacrifice,
Blood for this hope.
How deep this hour, like morning,
Happiness decorated
With the plain truth of spring!
And lives cross one another,
High, radiant lives.
Under the azure, suddenly ... Silence?
A cheer. Hurrah! The sudden ovation
For pure convergence in the sun.
A chorus? No. Better:
Common April on a united earth,
April!
All at once it is possible
To grow rich in joy for the mere sum
Of so much common joy,
For the stirring accumulation
Of clarity and hope.
In the air, a future
Free, free from death —
Or with life in death, further on.
Expectation of endless life
For me, for everyone,
An open path to the hours!
I shout to the sun, the flood, the plain of fiesta.
The multitude surges in its gaiety,
And all things are united again,
Fertile.
Everyone's hope!

JAMES WRIGHT

ADEMÁS

Júbilo al sol. ¿De quién? ¿De todos? Júbilo.

Un sonreír ya general apenas
De relumbre y penumbra se distingue.
Facilidad de acera matutina,
Deslizamiento de los carrüajes
Sin premura hacia un fondo de gran Mayo,
Supremo en la avenida tersamente
Dócil al resbalar de la mañana.
¿Por qué las calles tanto me embelesan
Si nada acciona como tentación
Por mi camino hermoso y cotidiano?
Penden tal vez más densos los follajes,
Olerá más al sol —recién cortada—
La hierba en los declives de un jardín.
¿O debo mi ventura al raudo ataque
—En una sola ráfaga de brisa
Como una embriaguez insostenible,
Si no es un solo instante— del aroma
Que hacia mi alma exhalan esos pinos?
¿O será nada más este calor,
Tan leve y ya tan abrazado al mundo?
Todo apunta hacia un ápice perfecto,
Y sin decir su perfección me colma

BESIDES

Praise be to the sun. Whose? Everybody's?
    Praise be.

The over-all smile scarcely distinguishes
Between the shimmer and the shadow.
The ease of the morning sidewalk,
The unhurried passing of carriages
Toward the vast far end of May,
Culminating in the avenue, smooth, gentle
Under the steps of the morning.
Why do the streets so draw me
When nothing odd tempts me
On my serene, everyday walk?
Perhaps the foliage hangs more thickly,
Perhaps the new-cut grass will smell
Even more of the sun on the slopes of some garden.
Or do I owe my luck to a sudden whiff –
In a single stir of the breeze
Like an overwhelming drug,
Beyond the moment – of the scent
Which those pines breathe into my soul?
This heat, so light, and yet
So laden with the world, will it
Be nothing more than it is?
Everything points to an apex of perfection
Which, without speaking, fills me

De la más clara fe primaveral.
¿Este suelo? Meseta en que me pasmo
De tanta realidad inmerecida,
Ocasión de mi júbilo. Tan firme,
Tan entrañable, tan viril lo siento
Que se confunde con mi propia esencia.
Hoy me asomo feliz a la mañana
Porque la vida corre con la sangre,
Y se me imponen placenteramente
Mi fatal respirar y un sonreír
Sin causa, porque sí, porque es mi sino
Propender con fervor al universo
—Quien, réplica dichosa de los dados,
Responde con prodigios además.
De veras se dirige a mi fervor
Esa luz sonriente en la penumbra
Del pavimento, bajo los follajes,
Sonriente en los claros de los troncos
Y de las hojas más privilegiadas,
Entre el verdor cortés y su ciudad.

Todo es prodigio por añadidura.

With the clearest faith in the spring.
This ground? A plateau on which
I astonish myself with a sense
Of such odd, intense reality,
The cause of my praise. So firm,
So deeply, so strong do I feel it
That I cannot tell it from my being.
Today I seem blessed by the morning,
For life runs at one with the blood,
And in sheer pleasure
I draw my fatal breath,
And smile without any reason,
Yes, for always my fate is
To tend to the world with joy –
Who, with the luck of the dice,
Answers with marvels besides.
It is truly aimed at my wonder,
That light which smiles in the shadows
Of sidewalks, under the foliage,
Smiles from the shine of the tree trunks,
And the leaves which the sun has chosen,
Between the graceful greenness and the city.

And all is marvelous, besides.

ALASTAIR REID

AMOR A UNA MAÑANA

Mañana, mañana clara:
¡Si fuese yo quien te amara!

Paso a paso en tu ribera,
Yo seré quien más te quiera.

Hacia toda tu hermosura
Mi palabra se apresura.

Henos sobre nuestra senda.
Déjame que yo te entienda.

¡Hermosura delicada
Junto al filo de la nada!

Huele a mundo verdadero
La flor azul del romero.

¿De tal lejanía es dueña
La malva sobre la peña?

Vibra sin cesar el grillo.
A su paciencia me humillo.

LOVE SONG TO A MORNING

Morning, clear morning,
If only I were your lover!

With every step I take on your margin,
I should long for you all the more.

My word hurries to gather
All of your fresh beauty.

Here we are, on our path.
Let me understand you.

Loveliness, held lightly
To the blade of nothingness!

The blue rosemary
Smells of the real earth.

How much of the world does the mallow
Grasp from her stone?

The cricket trills endlessly.
I bow to his patience.

¡Cuánto gozo a la flor deja
Preciosamente la abeja!

Y se zambulle, se obstina
La abeja. ¡Calor de mina!

El grillo ahora acelera
Su canto. ¿Más primavera?

Se pierde quien se lo pierde.
¡Qué mío el campo tan verde!

Cielo insondable a la vista:
Amor es quien te conquista.

¿No merezco tal mañana?
Mi corazón se la gana.

Claridad, potencia suma:
Mi alma en ti se consuma.

How much joy the honeybee
Leaves to the flower!

And he plunges, laboring
In the heat of the mine.

Now the cricket is hurrying
His song. Is there yet more spring?

Whoever loses all this, loses himself.
So much green, and the field mine!

Heaven that the eye cannot fathom:
It is love that wins you.

Don't I deserve such a morning?
My heart earns it.

Clarity, uttermost strength:
My soul is fulfilled in you.

JAMES WRIGHT

UNA VENTANA

El cielo sueña nubes para el mundo real
Con elemento amante de la luz y el espacio.
Se desparraman hoy dunas de un arrecife,
Arenales con ondas marinas que son nieves.
Tantos cruces de azar, por ornato caprichos,
Están ahí de bulto con una irresistible
Realidad sonriente. Yo resido en las márgenes
De una profundidad de trasparencia en bloque.
El aire está ciñendo, mostrando, realzando
Las hojas en la rama, las ramas en el tronco,
Los muros, los aleros, las esquinas, los postes:
Serenidad en evidencia de la tarde,
Que exige una visión tranquila de ventana.
Se acoge el pormenor a todo su contorno:
Guijarros, esa valla, más lejos un alambre.
Cada minuto acierta con su propia aureola,
¿O es la figuración que sueña este cristal?
Soy como mi ventana. Me maravilla el aire.
¡Hermosura tan límpida ya de tan entendida,
Entre el sol y la mente! Hay palabras muy tersas,

A WINDOW

The sky dreams its clouds for the actual world
With a lover's beginnings: light and the void.
The dunes scatter out in the shallows today,
Sand bars, with waves breaking landward, like snow.
Those chance countercrossings, vagrant embellishments
That mass for the eye with such sovereign
Reality and smile for us here. I dwell on the verge
Of transparency, deep in the heft of things.
Air circles the leaves, displaying the shapes
On the branches, the branch on the bole of the tree,
    making them real:
The line of a gable, corners and fenceposts and walls,
The manifest poise of the evening
That orders its dream of tranquillity there on the window.
The particular turns into itself with the whole of its
    contour:
Pebble and paling, a wire's span in the distance,
Each moment propounding its fated effulgency –
Or is it a windowpane's dream of configurement only?
I to myself am a window. Air stuns me to wonder.
The loveliness loosed in such limpid extension
Between light and enlightenment! There are terser
    locutions,

Y yo quiero saber como el aire de Junio.
La inquietud de algún álamo forma brisa visible,
En círculo de paz se me cierra la tarde,
Y un cielo bien alzado se ajusta a mi horizonte.

I would know as the wind knows in June.
A stir in the poplars, the visible cast of the breeze.
The afternoon closes me in with its peaceful encirclement
And the uttermost thrusts of the sky conform to my
    zenith.

BEN BELITT

ANILLO

I

Ya es secreto el calor, ya es un retiro
De gozosa penumbra compartida.
Ondea la penumbra. No hay suspiro
Flotante. Lo mejor soñado es vida.

¡Profunda tarde interna en el secreto
De una estancia que no se sabe dónde
—Tesoro igual con su esplendor completo—
Entre los rayos de la luz se esconde!

El vaivén de un silencio luminoso
Frunce entre las persianas una fibra
Palpitante. Querencia del reposo:
Una ilusión en el polvillo vibra.

Desde la sombra inmóvil la almohada
Brinda a los dos felices el verano
De una blancura tan afortunada
Que se convierte en sumo acorde humano.

Como una brisa orea la blancura.
Playa se tiende, playa se abandona.
Un afán más umbrío se aventura
Vagando por la playa y la persona.

RING

I

Here the heat grows secret, a refuge now
Of glad shadows that two lovers can share.
Flickering half-shadow. But not a human sigh
Floating anywhere. Our best dreams now come alive.

Indoors, deep afternoon in the secrecy
Of a chamber no one knows where –
Treasure always the same, with its splendor complete—
Has gone into hiding between the rays of light.

The flowing back and forth of a luminous silence
Twists a trembling fiber of light into threads
Between the window blinds. Haunt of repose:
The lovers' hope quivers in the motes of dust.

Out of the unmoving dark, the pillow
Offers the happy two a whole summer
Of a dazzling white so fortunate
That it is changed into highest human accord.

Like a flowing breeze the whiteness freshens the air.
The shore spreads out, the shore surrenders itself.
Now desire ventures eagerly toward the shadow,
Loitering on the shore and on the naked body.

Los dos felices, en las soledades
Del propio clima salvo del invierno,
Buscan en claroscuros sin edades
La refulgencia de un estío eterno.

Hay tanta plenitud en esta hora,
Tranquila entre las palmas de algún hado,
Que el curso del instante se demora
Lentísimo, cortés, enamorado.

Honda acumulación está por dentro
Levantando el nivel de una meseta,
Donde el presente ocupa y fija el centro
De tanta inmensidad así concreta.

Esa inquietud de sol por la tarima,
—Sol con ese zumbido de la calle
Que sitiando al silencio le reanima—
Esa ansiedad en torno al mismo talle,

Y de repente espacio libre, sierra,
A la merced de un viento que embriaga,
El viento más fragante que destierra
Todo vestigio de la historia aciaga,

¿Dónde están, cuándo ocurren? No hay historia.
Hubo un ardor que es este ardor. Un día
Solo, profundizado en la memoria,
A su eterno presente se confía.

The two that are happy, in the solitudes
Of their own climate, safe beyond any winter,
Search in the ageless weavings of light and shade
For the full radiance of eternal summer.

There is so much fullness in the present moment,
Tranquil between the palms of destiny's hands,
That the running course of one instant lingers,
Slowly, gracefully, delighted into love.

From within, profound accumulations
Are raising the level of a plateau,
Where the present moment fills and fixes the center
Of so much immensity, made solid now.

The restlessness of the sun on the wooden floor –
Sunlight with the murmuring of the street
That, besieging the silence, only encourages it –
This ardent desire circling the same figure,

And suddenly, free space, a sierra,
At the mercy of a wind that makes one drunk,
A fragrant wind that banishes from the earth
Every trace of unlucky history.

Where are these things, when do they happen?
   History is gone.
It had passion, it was *this* passion. One day
Alone, grown profound in the memory,
Entrusts itself to the present moment forever.

II

Aunque el deseo precipita un culto
Que es un tropel absorto, da un rodeo
Y en reverencia cambia su tumulto,
Sin cesar renaciente del deseo.

Sobre su cima la hermosura espera,
Y entregándose toda se recata
Lejos —¿cómo ideal y verdadera?—
Tan improbable aún y ya inmediata.

¡Es tan central así, tan absoluta
La Tierra bien sumida en universo,
Sin cesar tan creado! ¡Cuánta fruta
De una sazón en su contorno terso!

El amor está ahí, fiel Infinito
—No es posible el final— sobre el minuto
Lanzando de una vez, aerolito
Súbito, la agresión de lo absoluto.

¡Oh súbita dulzura! No hay sorpresa,
Tan soñado responde el gran contento.
Y por la carne acude el alma y cesa
La soledad del mundo en su lamento.

II

Although desire hurries a cult of worshipers
Into an ecstatic crowd, it strikes yet another road
And guides the tumult into reverence
Without hindering the rebirth of desire.

Womanly beauty waits upon the summit
And, yielding everything, acts with modesty
At a distance – how ideal, and how true˙ –
So improbable and yet so immediate.

It is so central to all, so absolute,
The earth utterly plunged in the universe,
So intensely created without ceasing! How much fruit,
In its smooth contour, exists in a single season!

Love is here – faithful Infinity
That cannot possibly end – all at once,
A sudden meteorite, launching
Its attack of the absolute.

O sudden sweetness! There is no surprise,
For the great gladness only fulfills the dream.
And the soul comes to uplift the flesh and to ease
The loneliness of the world in its lament.

¡Gozo de gozos: el alma en la piel,
Ante los dos el jardín inmortal,
El paraíso que es ella con él,
Óptimo el árbol sin sombra de mal!

Luz nada más. He ahí los amantes.
Una armonía de montes y ríos,
Amaneciendo en lejanos levantes,
Vuelve inocentes los dos albedríos.

¿Dónde estará la apariencia sabida?
¿Quién es quien surge? Salud, inmediato
Siempre, palpable misterio: presida
Forma tan clara a un candor de arrebato.

¿Es la hermosura quien tanto arrebata,
O en la terrible alegría se anega
Todo el impulso estival? (¡Oh beata
Furia del mar, esa ola no es ciega!)

Aun retozando se afanan las bocas,
Inexorables a fuerza de ruego.
(Risas de Junio, por entre unas rocas,
Turban el límpido azul con su juego.)

¿Yace en los brazos un ansia agresiva?
Calladamente resiste el acorde.
(¡Cuánto silencio de mar allá arriba!
Nunca hay fragor que el cantil no me asorde.)

III

Joy of joys: the spirit under the skin,
And before the lovers the garden that lives always,
A paradise created out of woman and man,
The tree – supremely good – casting no shadow of evil!

Nothing except light. Here are the lovers.
A sweet harmony of mountains and rivers
Dawning in the far distances of the east
Turns innocent the two free wills.

Where do they put on their ordinary appearance?
Who is it surges here? Welcome, immediate
Yet lasting, mystery solid in the hands: may a form
So clear preside over an innocence of rapture.

Is it woman's beauty that is so captivating?
Or is it the whole urge of summer that drowns
In a terrible happiness? (O blessed
Fury of the sea, this wave is not blind!)

Still frolicking, their mouths toil eagerly,
Inexorable with the power of entreaty.
(The laughters of June among the rocks
Shatter the limpid blue with their games.)

Does an aggressive urge rest in their arms?
Softly, silently, harmony resists.
(How much of the sea's stillness there is, up there!
Not a crash that the cliff does not silence.)

Y se encarnizan los dos violentos
En la ternura que los encadena.
(El regocijo de los elementos
Torna y retorna a la última arena.)

Ya las rodillas, humildes aposta,
Saben de un sol que al espíritu asalta.
(El horizonte en alturas de costa
Llega a la sal de una brisa más alta.)

¡Felicidad! El alud de un favor
Corre hasta el pie, que retuerce su celo.
(Cruje el azul. Sinuoso calor
Va alabeando la curva del cielo.)

Gozo de ser: el amante se pasma.
¡Oh derrochado presente inaudito,
Oh realidad en raudal sin fantasma!
Todo es potencia de atónito grito.

Alrededor se consuma el verano.
Es un anillo la tarde amarilla.
Sin una nube desciende el cercano
Cielo a este ardor. ¡Sobrehumana, la arcilla!

And those violent two clutch at each other
In the tenderness that links them together.
(And the rejoicing of the elements
Turning, turning again, at the edge of the sand.)

Their knees, arranged humbly now on purpose,
Know of a sun that assaults the spirit.
(The salt breath of a high breeze reaches
To the horizon on the heights of the coast.)

Happiness! The avalanche of the act of love
Slides clear to the feet, twisting them into fire.
(The azure creaks. A sinuous warmth
Goes warping the curve of the sky.)

Joy of being: the lover lies in his spasm.
O extraordinary present, spent now.
O reality, O torrent in full flesh!
Everything is a latent astonished cry.

On every hand the summer reaches its consummation.
The yellow afternoon is a circle.
Without a cloud the neighboring sky descends
On this passion. This clay, more than human.

IV

¡Gloria de dos! —sin que la dicha estorbe
Su repliegue hacia el resto de lo oscuro.
En torno de la almohada ronda el orbe,
Vive la flor sobre el papel del muro.

Un cansancio común se comunica
Por el tendido cuerpo con el alma,
Que se tiende también a solas rica,
Ya en posesión de aquella doble calma.

¡Es un reposo de tan dulce peso,
Que con tanta molicie cae, cede,
Se hunde, profundiza el embeleso
De dos destinos en la misma sede!

Hombres hay que destrozan en barullo
Tristísimo su voz y sus entrañas.
Sin embargo . . . ¿No escuchas el arrullo
Reparador del aire entre las cañas?

¡El aire! Vendaval o viento o brisa,
Resonando o callando, siempre existe
Su santa desnudez. ¿No la divisa
Con los ojos de un dios hasta el más triste?

IV

Glory of two! But without letting happiness hinder
Their retreat toward the rest of darkness.
The whole globe circles around their pillow,
The flower on the wallpaper springs alive.

A common weariness places the outspread
Body in touch with the soul,
That also lies outspread, richly alone,
Already possessor of that twofold calm.

This is a repose of so sweet a burden,
Tumbling so softly down, yielding,
Sinking further, finally deepening the delight
Of two destinies in a single place.

Some men shatter their voices and rend themselves
Deep inside in melancholy confusion.
Nevertheless . . . Can you hear the healing
Lullaby of the air in the tall reeds?

The air! Terrible gale or wind or breeze,
Resounding or falling into a hush, always its pure
Nakedness exists. Doesn't even the saddest man
Perceive it, as though with the eyes of a god?

V

Y se sumerge todo el ser, tranquilo
Con vigor, en la paz del universo,
La enorme paz que da a la guerra asilo,
Todo en más vasta pleamar inmerso.

Irresistible creación redonda
Se esparce universal como una gana,
Como una simpatía de onda en onda
Que se levanta en esperanza humana.

Arroyo claro sobre peña y guijo:
¿Para morir no quieres detenerte?
Amor en creación, en flor, en hijo:
¿Adónde vas sin miedo de la muerte?

Hermoso tanto espacio ante la cumbre,
Amor es siempre vida, sólo vida.
No hay mirada amorosa que no alumbre
Su eternidad. Allí secreta anida.

¡Oh presente sin fin, ahora eterno
Con frescura continua de rocío,
Y sin saber del mal ni del invierno,
Absoluto en su cámara de estío!

¡Increíble absoluto en esa mina
Que halla el amor —buscándose a lo largo
De un tiempo en marcha siempre hacia su ruina—
A la cabeza del vivir amargo!

V

And the lovers' whole being, tranquil in its strength,
Sinks back into the peace of the universe,
The enormous peace that gives shelter from war,
Everything gathered into the huge tide.

The irresistible circle of creation
Spreads out over the universe like a great longing,
Like the sympathy of wave falling on wave
That is uplifted into a human hope.

Clear stream over the stone and gravel:
Don't you want to pause on your way to dying?
Love in creation, in flowers, in children:
Where are you going without fear of death?

How beautiful so much space before the summit!
Love is always life, it is only life.
There is no gaze of love that does not give birth
To its eternity. It nests there, in secret.

O endless present, now that lasts forever
With the continual freshness of the dew,
And, knowing nothing of evil or of winter,
Absolute in this inner chamber of summer!

Incredible absolute, hidden in this mine
That love discovers — searching along
In the midst of time that marches toward its ruin —
Guiding our difficult life!

Tanto presente, de verdad, no pasa.
Feliz el río, que pasando queda.
¡Oh tiempo afortunado! Ved su casa.
Este amor es fortuna ya sin rueda.

Bien ocultos por voces y por gestos,
Ágiles a pesar de tanto lazo,
Viven los dos gozosamente opuestos
Entre las celosías de su abrazo.

En la penumbra el rayo no descansa.
La amplitud de la tarde ciñe inmensa.
Bajo el secreto de una luz tan mansa,
Amor solar se logra y se condensa.

Y se yerguen seguros dos destinos
Afrontando la suerte de los días,
Pedregosos tal vez o diamantinos.
Todos refulgirán, Amor, si guías.

¡Sea la tarde para el sol! La Tierra
No girará con trabazón más fuerte.
En torno a un alma el círculo se cierra.
¿Por vencida te das ahora, Muerte?

So much of the present, truly, cannot pass.
Happy the river that, passing, yet remains.
O fortunate time! Let us see your house.
This love is already lucky, without fortune's wheel.

Concealed by voices and by gestures,
Nimble still in spite of so many bonds,
The lovers live joyously on, two contraries,
Between the tangling lattices of their embrace.

In the deep shade the sun's rays still move.
The breadth of the immense afternoon is circling.
Beneath the secret of a light so gentle,
Love under the sun flourishes and grows strong.

And they stand upright, secure, two destinies
Confronting the chance of the days,
Sometimes stony, sometimes like a diamond.
All days will shine, Love, if you are their guide.

May the afternoon be the sun's. The earth
Will never spin upon a stronger brace.
The circle closes itself around the spirit.
Now do you surrender, Death?

JAMES WRIGHT

DESNUDO

Blancos, rosas. Azules casi en veta,
    Retraídos, mentales.
Puntos de luz latente dan señales
    De una sombra secreta.

Pero el color, infiel a la penumbra,
    Se consolida en masa.
Yacente en el verano de la casa,
    Una forma se alumbra.

Claridad aguzada entre perfiles,
    De tan puros tranquilos,
Que cortan y aniquilan con sus filos
    Las confusiones viles.

Desnuda está la carne. Su evidencia
    Se resuelve en reposo.
Monotonía justa, prodigioso
    Colmo de la presencia.

¡Plenitud inmediata, sin ambiente,
    Del cuerpo femenino!
Ningún primor: ni voz ni flor. ¿Destino?
    ¡Oh absoluto Presente!

NUDE

Whites, pinks. Barely a vein of blue,
    Remote, guessed.
High points of latent light suggest
    A secret in the shadow.

But the color, hazy at its limit,
    Intensifies in the mass.
Deep in the summer of the house,
    A form springs to light.

Such quiet purity of outline
    Sharpening the clarity of it –
Profiles whose clean edges cut
    Across all confusion.

The flesh is naked. Just what it is
    Grows clear in its repose.
An exact monotony, the enormous
    Overflowing of a presence.

The separate, sure, immediate fullness
    Of a woman's body! Not the grace,
Nor flower, nor voice. But to what purpose?
    The absolute Present! This!

ALASTAIR REID

EL CONCIERTO

El tiempo se divide resonando.
¡Ah! Se levanta un mundo
Que vale, se me impone, me subyuga
Con su necesidad.
Es así. Justamente,
Según esta delicia de rigor,
Ha de ser en el aire:
Un mundo
Donde yo llego a respirar con todos
Mis silencios acordes.

Sumiso a ese fluir de voluntad,
Escucho.
Mi atención es mi alma.
Convivo
Con esta convergencia de energías
En su resolución.
¿Qué dice, qué propone?
Se propone, se muestra,
Se identifica a su absoluto ser.

Absoluto de instantes,
El uno para el otro ya inminente.

THE CONCERT

Time divides and resonates.
Ah! A world of value comes to life,
Marks me, and submits me
To its necessity.
So. Exactly,
With just this precision of delight,
It will come to pass in the air:
A world
Where I begin to breathe with all
My silences in tune.

I yield to this flowing in my will.
I listen.
My soul is my attentiveness.
I am one
With this converging of excitement
As it resolves.
What is it saying, or suggesting?
It suggests itself, it reveals itself.
It becomes its own pure being.

Entirety of separate moments,
Each one dawning from the other.

Todo el ser en fluencia,
De sonido a intervalo situado.
Y todo se desliza,
Coexiste seguro, deleitable,
—!Qué espera, qué tensión, qué altura ya!—
Mientras en la memoria permanece,
Confín de mi placer,
Una totalidad de monumento.

En su temple el espíritu,
Desde su cima escucha,
Más fuerte, más agudo
Que abajo,
Entre arrugas y ruidos.
Escucha un hombre sin querer ya nuevo,
Ya interior a ese coto de armonía
Que envuelve como el aire:
Con mi vivir se funde.
¿Con mi propio vivir?
¿Ahora seré yo,
Yo mismo a mi nivel,
Quien vive con el puro firmamento?
Me perteneces, música,
Dechado sobrehumano
Que un hombre entrega al hombre.

No hay discordia posible.
El acaso jamás en este círculo
Puede irrumpir, crujir:

All being flowing
From note to careful interval.
Everything slips away,
Yet stays, is there, exquisitely –
The hope, the tension, the climax still –
While in the memory,
The enclosure of my pleasure, remains
A monumental wholeness.

The spirit moves in its temper,
Listening, from its distance,
Stronger, more acute there
Than in the world below,
Rumpled and noisy.
A man without longings listens, renewed now,
Held now in the confines of this harmony,
Enfolding him like air;
It fuses with my life.
With my true life?
Will I now be
I myself, at my true level,
Someone who lives in purest air?
Music, you involve me,
As a more than human instance
Which one man transmits to another.

Discord is not possible.
In this pure circle, accident
Can never break or contradict:

Orbe en manos y en mente
De hacedor que del todo lo realiza.
¡Oh música,
Suprema realidad!
Es el despliegue mismo
—Oíd— de un firmamento
—Lo veis— que nos recoge.
Nada sonoro ocurre
Fuera. Ya ¿dónde estamos?

(Música y suerte: cámara
De amigos.
La tarde es el gran ámbito.
Aliada a través de las vidrieras,
Profunda,
Consagrándose a estar,
Estando,
Sin oír nos atiende.
¿Tal vez culmina aquí
La final amistad del universo?
Muy diáfana la atmósfera,
Arboleda en un fondo de balcones,
Las ondas del nogal en la penumbra
De ese mueble, tarima sin crujido,
Un tono general, acompañante.
Seguro este presente.)

¿Dónde, por dónde estamos?
Me sostiene una cumbre

A globe being realized
In the hands and mind of the maker.
O music,
The utmost reality !
It is the actual unfolding –
Listen ! – of a world –
See it? – which draws us in.
Nothing can sound
Outside it. But now where are we?

(Music and luck : a room
Of friends.
The confines are the afternoon.
Joined across the glass,
Profound,
Devoting itself to existence,
Existing,
Unhearing, it attends us.
Will this be perhaps the final
Culmination of all friendship?
Diaphanous the atmosphere,
A grove in a recess of balconies,
Waves of walnut in the aura
Of this woodwork, the soundlessness of the floor,
An over-all tone, accompanying.
Safe, sure is this present.)

But where? Where are we?
This pinnacle sustains me,

—Sobre cualquier lugar. ¿Qué pide el ritmo?
No responde a su anhelo, no se basta
Con toda su belleza ineludible,
Y torna con retorno que suplica,
Tal vez a mí buscándome.
El alma se abalanza a ese compás,
Que es alma.

¡Oh Bien! Y se desnuda.
Le siento sin ideas, sin visiones,
Reveladoramente,
Nada más por contacto
Con mi naturaleza,
Que acompasada ahonda en su vivir,
En su dominio o su melancolía,
En este ser ahora tan entero,
Tan firme que es de todos.
¡Ninguna confidencia!
La sucesión de sones,
Jamás en soledad,
Sin ruptura de olvido,
Pasa relacionando el gran conjunto
—Donde trascurre incógnito el oyente,
Solidario en alerta.

Alerta dominada.
¡Música, poderío!
Y me fía a sus cúspides,
Me colma de su fe,

Whatever the place beneath. What is the rhythm
   asking?
Not meeting its own longings, not content
With all its unavoidable beauty,
Turning and returning in supplication,
Seeking, seeking me, perhaps.
The spirit falling into this measure
Which is spirit.

Well-being! Yes! And it strips itself naked.
I feel it void of idea or vision,
As revelation,
Pure in its contact
With my own nature,
Arranging the founds of my being,
Its force, its melancholy;
In it, I feel my wholeness,
So firmly at one with the world.
Nothing is confidential!
The sounds in relation,
Never separated,
Or broken by forgetting,
Draw all things into a whole –
There is where listening happens, unaware,
Blending into attention.

A controlled attention.
Music, the power of it!
And I trust in its pinnacles,
Its faith overwhelms me,

Me erige en su esplendor,
Sobre el último espacio conquistable,
Me tiende a su ondear de creaciones,
Junto al más fresco arranque de alegría,
Me expone frente a frente
De la gran realidad en evidencia,
Y con su certidumbre me embriaga.
¡Armonía triunfante!
Imperando persiste,
Hermosamente espíritu.
Es él, es él, es todo su inmediato
Caudal.

En una gloria aliento.
Porque tanto se eleva sobre mí,
Perfección superior a toda vida
Me rige.
¡Oh música del hombre y más que el hombre,
Último desenlace
De la audaz esperanza!

Suena, música, suena,
Exáltame a la orilla,
Ráptame al interior
De la ventura que en el día mío
Levantas.
Remontado al concierto
De esta culminación de realidad,
Participo también de tu victoria:
Absoluta armonía en aire humano.

Its splendor sustains me
Beyond the furthest recesses of space.
It draws me into the sway of its creations
With the freshest impulse of joy,
It exposes me, face to face,
To the enormity of reality,
And I am dizzy with its sureness.
Triumphant harmony!
It commands insistently,
The spirit, most beautifully.
It, it, in all its tangible
Abundance.

In glory, a reviving.
For now, a greatness awes me,
And a perfection beyond life
Is moving me.
Music, man's music, and yet so much more than
    man!
The last unfolding
Of breathless hope!

Sound then, music. Sound
And exalt me to my limit,
Carry me deep into the wonder
Which in this day of mine you awaken.
Realizing the concert
Of this culminating reality,
I too join in your victory:
The perfection of harmony occurring in human
    air.   ALASTAIR REID

CABALLOS EN EL AIRE

(CINEMATÓGRAFO)

Caballos.
Lentísimos partiendo y ya en el aire,
¿Van a volar tal vez?

La atmósfera se agrisa.
¡Cuánto más resistente
Su espesura más gris!
Con lentitud y precaución de tacto
Las patas se despliegan
Avanzando a través
De una tarde de luna.
Muy firme la cabeza pero sorda,
Más y más retraída a su silencio,
Las crines siempre inmóviles
Y muy tendido el lomo,
Los caballos ascienden.
¿Vuelan tal vez sin un temblor de ala
Por un aire de luna?
Y sin contacto con la tierra torpe,
Las patas a compás
—¿Dentro de qué armonía?—
Se ciernen celestiales,
A fuerza de abandono misteriosas.

HORSES IN THE AIR

(MOTION PICTURE)

Horses.
Lightest of leave-takings, treading air now,
Intent upon flight – is it possible?

The weather goes ashen.
How unyieldingly now
The bulk of that grayness increases itself !
Circumspect and deliberate, trying the way
With their hoofprints, the horses deploy,
Pressing on
Through the moon of the midday.
Their ever more resolute heads, now muted,
Withdrawn more and more in their silence,
The manes never moving
And the haunches strained taut,
The horses vault upward.
Can it be they are climbing the lunar ascents
Of the air without beating a feather?
Never touching earth's torpor,
The hooves, keeping measure –
In the hold of what harmony? –
Lunge toward their heaven,
Spurred waywardly upward, mysterious.

¿O a fuerza de cuidado?
Inútiles, se entregan los jinetes
—¿Para qué ya las bridas?—
A las monturas suaves y sonámbulas,
Que a una atracción de oscuridad cediendo
Se inclinan otra vez hacia la tierra,
Sólo por fin rozada
Sin romper el prodigio,
Rebotando, volando a la amplitud
Sin cesar fascinante.

Avanzan y no miran los caballos.
Y un caballo tropieza.
¡Con qué sinuosidad de cortesía
Roza, cae, se dobla,
Se doblega a lo oscuro,
Se tiende en su silencio!
Hay más blanco en los ojos.
Más aceradamente se difunden
Los grises
Sobre el inmóvil estupor del mundo.
Las manchas de gentío
Se borran
Tras vallados penosos
Con su oscura torpeza de rumores.
Los caballos ascienden, bajan, pisan,
Pisan un punto, parten,
A ciegas tan certeros,

Or does some deeper solicitude drive them?
Unpurposed, the riders abandon themselves –
What can their bridles constrain for them now? –
To the bland and somnambulant horses
Impelled by a shadow's attraction,
Bending earthward again, a little
Unsteady of pace in the end,
Never marring the miracle,
Rebounding, soaring up into air's
Inexhaustible sorcery.

The horses advance, turning nowhere to look.
And one of them stumbles.
With what twining civility
He falters and falls, bows himself double,
Surrenders himself to the darkness
And stretches his length in the silence !
The eyeballs are whiter.
And all that was gray now diffuses
A steelier color
On the motionless trance of a world.
The stain of the multitude
Clouds in
On the thorny enclosures
With the shadowy sloth of its murmur.
The horses ascend and descend, tread onward,
Tread on, a degree at a time, and divide,
Blindly, unerringly,

Más sordos cada vez, flotantes, leves,
Pasando, resbalando.
¡Qué ajuste sideral
De grises,
Qué tino de fantasmas
Para llegar a ser
Autómatas de cielo,
Espíritus —estrellas en su trance
Seguro sin premura!

¿Sin premura de fondo?
Esta pasión de lentitud ahora
¿No es todavía rápida,
No fue ya rapidez?
Rapidez en segundos manifiesta.
Visibles y tangibles,
Desmenuzan el vértigo
De antes
En aquel interior de torbellino:
Corpúsculos, segundos, arenisca
De la más lenta realidad compacta.

¡Gracia de este recóndito sosiego!
El animal se cierne,
Espíritu por fin,
Sobre praderas fáciles.
¡Allá abajo el obstáculo
Sobre el suelo de sombra!

Deafened with changes, afloat in their buoyancy,
Pacing and gliding.
What a starry concession
Of grayness,
How adept in their fantasies,
Who emerge
As the heaven's automatons,
Pure spirit – catalept stars
Secure in their orbit, unhurrying.

Unhurried and whole – to their depths?
That rage for the gradual – even now,
Are its speeds not upon us,
Did we not feel its passing as speed?
Speed clusters its seconds:
Palpable, visible,
They demolish the dizzy
Precedence
In the eye of that whirlwind.
Sandmotes and corpuscles, the passing of seconds,
Compact in the dawdling reality.

O grace of that recondite calm!
The animal soars,
Pure spirit, at last,
Over effortless meadows.
Past all impediments there
Over the floor of the darkness!

Silencio. Los rumores del gentío
Por entre las cornisas y las ramas
Desaparecerán,
Callarán los insectos entre hierbas
Enormes,
Y follajes de hierro
Se habrán forjado a solas.
Alguna flor allí
Revelará sus pétalos en grande.

¡Qué lentitud en ser!
Corred, corred, caballos.
Implacable, finísima,
La calma permanece.
¡Cuántas fieles ayudas primorosas
A espaldas de la prisa!
Envolviendo en su gris
Discurre la paciencia
Por entre los corpúsculos del orbe,
Y con su red se extiende
Sobre las lentas zonas resguardadas.
Entre una muchedumbre de segundos
Se ocultan, aparecen
Los cuerpos estelares
—Y esos caballos solos,
Arriba solos sobre el panorama.
¡Cascos apenas, leves y pulidos
Pedruscos!

Silence. The chattering pack
In the branches and cornices
Fades,
The insects are dumb in the towering
Grasses,
And a leafage of iron
Will forge itself out of the solitude.
A flower
Will display all the breadth of its petals.

How gradual, our coming to be!
Horses, make haste, hasten on!
Exquisite, implacable,
The serenity stays.
How compliant and perfect, all the succor
That waits for us there, beyond haste!
Immersed in its grayness,
A patience flows forth
Among particles locked in the orb
And enlarges its mesh
In the gradual zones, without hazard.
In a thronging of seconds
All the bodily stars
Withhold and display themselves –
And those horses, alone in the air,
Aloft and alone on the spread panorama.
Weightless and radiant rock splinters, potsherds.
Hardly more than that!

Entre los cielos van
Caballos estelares.
¿Caballos?

There in the heavens
The running of horses like stars.
Horses, then? Horses?

BEN BELITT

III

THE BIRD IN THE HAND

It is another instrument that enchants
The highest senses.

DON LUIS DE GÓNGORA

Permanece el trote aquí,
Entre su arranque y mi mano.
Bien ceñida queda así
Su intención de ser lejano.
Porque voy en un corcel
A la maravilla fiel:
Inmóvil con todo brío.
¡Y a fuerza de cuánta calma
Tengo en bronce toda el alma,
Clara en el cielo del frío!

EQUESTRIAN STATUE

See how the trot endures
Between his great leap forward and my hand;
And see how firmly reined
Is the instinct to gallop away.
Because the steed that I ride
Keeps faith with a marvel:
Motionless, he, yet charged with vigor.
And thanks to how deep a calm
I possess, in bronze, my soul entire,
Serene in a chilly sky.

BARBARA HOWES

Queda curvó el firmamento,
Compacto azul, sobre el día.
Es el redondeamiento
Del esplendor: mediodía.
Todo es cúpula. Reposa,
Central sin querer, la rosa,
A un sol en cenit sujeta.
Y tanto se da el presente
Que el pie caminante siente
La integridad del planeta.

PERFECTION

Curved, the firmament remains
Densely blue, above the day.
It moves toward that encircling
Of magnificence: midday.
All is a dome. Quietly
There at the center rests the rose,
Subject of the noonday sun.
And so much does the moment lend
That the traveling foot can feel
The completeness of the planet.

BARBARA HOWES

Yacente a solas, no está afligido, no está preso,
Pacificado al fin entre tierra y más tierra,
El esqueleto sin angustia, a solas hueso.
¡Descanse en paz, sin nosotros, bajo nuestra guerra!

CEMETERY

Neither grieving nor imprisoned but lying alone
Quiet at last between earth and still more
Earth: the unsuffering skeleton, made bone.
Rest peacefully, freed of our presences, under our war.

NORMAN THOMAS DI GIOVANNI

AMOR DORMIDO

Dormías, los brazos me tendiste y por sorpresa
Rodeaste mi insomnio. ¿Apartabas así
La noche desvelada, bajo la luna presa?
Tu soñar me envolvía, soñado me sentí.

LOVE SLEEPING

You lay sleeping, your arms held me, and almost to
    startle me,
You encircled my sleeplessness. Was it thus you dispelled
All the vigils of darkness in the moon's immobility?
Your dreaming encompassed me: I felt myself dreamed.

BEN BELITT

UNOS CABALLOS

Peludos, tristemente naturales,
En inmovilidad de largas crines
Desgarbadas, sumisos a confines
Abalanzados por los herbazales,

Unos caballos hay. No dan señales
De asombro, pero van creciendo afines
A la hierba. Ni bridas ni trajines.
Se atienen a su paz: son vegetales.

Tanta acción de un destino acaba en alma.
Velan soñando sombras las pupilas,
Y asisten, contribuyen a la calma

De los cielos —si a todo ser cercanos,
Al cuadrúpedo ocultos— las tranquilas
Orejas. Ahí están: ya sobrehumanos.

THE HORSES

Shaggy and heavily natural, they stand
Immobile under their thick and cumbrous manes,
Pent in a barbed enclosure which contains,
By way of compensation, grazing land.

Nothing disturbs them now. In slow increase
They fatten like the grass. Doomed to be idle,
To haul no cart or wagon, wear no bridle,
They grow into a vegetable peace.

Soul is the issue of so strict a fate.
They harbor visions in their waking eyes,
And with their quiet ears participate
In heaven's pure serenity, which lies
So near all things — yet from the beasts concealed.
Serene now, superhuman, they crop their field.

RICHARD WILBUR

MUERTE A LO LEJOS

Je soutenais l'éclat de la mort toute pure

VALÉRY

Alguna vez me angustia una certeza,
Y ante mí se estremece mi futuro.
Acechándole está de pronto un muro
Del arrabal final en que tropieza

La luz del campo. ¿Mas habrá tristeza
Si la desnuda el sol? No, no hay apuro
Todavía. Lo urgente es el maduro
Fruto. La mano ya le descorteza.

. . .Y un día entre los días el más triste
Será. Tenderse deberá la mano
Sin afán. Y acatando el inminente

Poder diré sin lágrimas: embiste,
Justa fatalidad. El muro cano
Va a imponerme su ley, no su accidente.

DEATH, FROM A DISTANCE

Je soutenais l'éclat de la mort toute pure

VALÉRY

When that dead certainty appalls my thought,
My future trembles on the road ahead.
There where the light of country fields is caught
In the blind, final precinct of the dead,
A wall takes aim.

              But what is sad, stripped bare
By the sun's gaze? It does not matter now —
Not yet. What matters is the ripened pear
That even now my hand strips from the bough.

The time will come: my hand will reach, some day,
Without desire. That saddest day of all,
I shall not weep, but with a proper awe
For the great force impending, I shall say,
*Lay on, just destiny. Let the white wall
Impose on me its uncapricious law.*

RICHARD WILBUR

163

VOCACIÓN DE SER

¡La mañana!
El olor a intemperie con rocío se ensancha,

Busca espacio
Virgen, profundidad en viento irrespirado,

Y la hierba
Recién aparecida, asomándose apenas

Con su verde
Pueril a los terrones que una gracia remueve,

De una vez
Extrema en elatónito su vocación de ser.

Morning!
The odor of outdoors spreads with the dew,

Looks for
Virgin space, profundity in wind unbreathed,

And the grass
Newly sprouted, barely beginning to appear

With its fresh
Green through a soil that gracefully yields,

Suddenly
Astonishes the onlooker with its vocation of being.

MARK STRAND

Noche mucho más noche : el amor ya es un hecho.
Feliz nivel de paz extiende el sueño
Como una perfección todavía amorosa.
Bulto adorable, lejos
Ya, se adormece,
Y a su candor en isla se abandona,
Animal por ahí, latente.
¡Qué diario Infinito sobre el lecho
De una pasión : costumbre rodeada de arcano !
¡Oh noche, más oscura en nuestros brazos !

Night is much more itself: love is already a fact.
The calm level of peace extends sleep
Like a perfection of love.
And love's bundle,
Now distant in sleep,
Abandons itself to an island of candor
Still keeping its animal nature.
What an infinity of days over the bed
Of one passion: habit surrounded by mystery!
O night, darker than ever in our arms!

MARK STRAND

Los ruidos tararean un susurro
Que ya en su cielo sonaría a canto.
Susurro aquí, resbala
Sobre el sol de las once suavizándose.
Creo en la maravilla suficiente
De esta calle a las once,
Cuando la vida arrecia
Con robustez normal, dichosa casi,
Humilde, realizada.
Las once son, la maravilla es tuya.

MIDMORNING

In its heaven this murmur of street noises
Might sound like song. But here
Gliding toward the eleven o'clock sun
It manages only to soften itself.
I believe in the sufficient marvel
Of this street at eleven,
When life picks up
With normal vigor, almost happy,
Humble, fulfilled.
Eleven o'clock, the marvel is yours.

MARK STRAND

Es una maravilla respirar lo más claro.
Veo a través del aire la inocencia absoluta,
Y si la luz se posa como una paz sin peso,
El alma es quien gravita con creciente volumen.
Todo se rinde al ánimo de un sosiego imperioso.
A mis ojos tranquilos más blancura da el muro,
Entre esas rejas verdes lo diario es lo bello,
Sobre la mies la brisa como una forma ondula,
Hasta el silencio impone su limpidez concreta.
Todo me obliga a ser centro del equilibrio.

EQUILIBRIUM

It is a marvel to breathe clarity.
I see complete innocence aslant the air;
And if light rests its burden like weightless peace,
Then is the soul borne down by its own blooming.
With a proud calm all things submit to the soul.
A wall is far more white to the tranquil eye,
Through this green grating the everyday has beauty,
Over the grain the breezes flow like forms,
Till silence interposes a solid clearness:
And all this brings me to equilibrium.

BARBARA HOWES

IV

HERE, NOW

This is no weary philosophy,
Sly transmutation nor vain alchemy,
But a real essence demanding to be touched.

LOPE

DESPERTAR

Nada. Tinieblas muelles.
Y de un golpe . . . ¿Qué, quién?

Restauración por vértigo,
Brusca restauración en aquel bulto
Que estaba así negándose,
Dulcemente dormido.

Negándose. ¿Negado?
Por la memoria alboreada irrumpe,
Vertical y de súbito,
Una abertura hacia el vacío.
¿Es una sima?
Sima . . . ¿De dónde?
Aquel bulto se siente ser, no está.
Casi ahogándose cae, cae. ¿Cuándo?

Y una angustia, relámpago en albor,
Ilumina el olvido y su desierto.
El atónito cae, se detiene.

Yo. Yo ahora. Yo aquí.
Despertar, ser, estar:
Otra vez el ajuste prodigioso.

WAKING

Nothingness . . . Tenuous shadow . . .
And all at once . . . What is it? Who?

Poise after vertigo,
Poise suddenly there in the shambles
That sought to disclaim itself so,
Peacefully sleeping.

Self-denying. Denied, rather?
There breaks forth, in a sunburst of memory,
Upright on that instant
A fissure that opens on vacancy.
A cavern, perhaps?
A cavern . . . But where?
A chaos is coming to be, not yet here.
It plunges, almost to drowning it plunges. But
    when – ?

And an agony, that bolt of the morning, lights
Oblivion's wilderness way.
While the astonished one plunges downward – and
    ceases to plunge –

And is I. Myself at this moment. Myself in this place.
I waken. I am. I exist.
Once again, O divine adaptation!

                            BEN BELITT

LA NIEVE

Lo blanco está sobre lo verde,
Y canta.
Nieve que es fina quiere
Ser alta.

Enero se alumbra con nieve, si verde,
Si blanca.
Que alumbre de día y de noche la nieve,
La nieve más clara.

¡Nieve ligera, copo blando,
Cuánto ardor en masa!
La nieve, la nieve en las manos
Y el alma.

Tan puro el ardor en lo blanco,
Tan puro, sin llama.
La nieve, la nieve hasta el canto
Se alza.

Enero se alumbra con nieve silvestre.
¡Cuánto ardor! Y canta.
La nieve hasta el canto —la nieve, la nieve—
En vuelo arrebata.

SNOW

White lies over green,
And it sings.
Snow that is delicate, snow that is light,
Longs to be deep.

January kindles to snow, is green
And is white.
May the blaze of the snow through the day
And the night kindle a lucider snow!

Delicate downfall, temperate flake,
What rage is made whole here!
It is snow: snow on the hands,
Snow on the soul.

So flawless the rage of that whiteness,
So flawless and flameless,
Snow bears itself upward, snow
Mounts and is song.

January burns rural with snow.
The rage of it! And it sings.
It touches its singing – snow upon snow upon
    snow –
In a headlong ascending of wings.

                           BEN BELITT

MÁS VERDAD

I

Sí, más verdad,
Objeto de mi gana.

¡Jamás, jamás engaños escogidos!

¿Yo escojo? Yo recojo
La verdad impaciente,
Esa verdad que espera a mi palabra.

¿Cumbre? Sí, cumbre
Dulcemente continua hasta los valles:
Un rugoso relieve entre relieves.
Todo me asombra junto.

Y la verdad
Hacia mí se abalanza, me atropella.

¡Más sol!
Venga ese mundo soleado,
Superior al deseo
Del fuerte,
Venga más sol feroz.

¡Más, más verdad!

MORE TRUTH

I

Yes, more truth
Is what I desire.

And not fine imitations!

Must I choose? No.
The truth is here
And eagerly awaits my word.

Is it a peak? Yes, a peak
That falls neatly into valleys:
A wrinkled relief among reliefs.
All of it amazes me.

And the truth
Rushes toward me, tramples me.

More sun!
Let that sun-drenched world come,
More powerful
Than might.
Let the sun pour down!

More, more truth!

Intacta bajo el sol de tantos hombres,
Esencial realidad,
Te sueño frente a frente,
De día,
Fuera de burladeros.
Eres tú quien alumbra
Mi predisposición de enamorado,
Mis tesoros de imágenes,
Esta mi claridad
O júbilo
De ser en la cadena de los seres,
De estar aquí.

El santo suelo piso.
Así, pisando, gozo
De ser mejor,
De sentir que voy siendo en plenitud,
A plomo gravitando humildemente
Sobre las realidades poseídas,
Soñadas por mis ojos y mis manos,
Por mi piel y mi sangre,
Entre mi amor y el horizonte cierto.

Son prodigios de tierra.

II

Essential reality,
Intact under the sun of all mankind,
In my dreams I face you,
By day,
All barriers down.
You bring to light
My lover's instinct,
My wealth of images,
My glory
Or joy
Of being in the chain of the living,
Of being here.

I stand on solid ground
And enjoy
A sense of elevation,
Of being more complete,
Of tending humbly toward
Realities already mine,
Dreamed by my eyes and hands,
By my skin and blood,
Between my love and the constant horizon.

They are the wonders of earth.

MARK STRAND

LAS NINFAS

En alto a solas, buscan
Aquel fulgor de un sol
Que las quisiera puras.

Y, gloria, la terraza
Levantará recién
Perfecta su mañana.

¡Cielos ya las alturas
Populosas de luz
Sin cortes ni penumbras!

Y la beldad resalta
Como una forma afín
A su interna esperanza.

Más: asciende a fortuna
Mayor de realidad
La carne así desnuda.

THE NYMPHS

They seek, high and alone,
That brilliance of a sun
Which would prefer them pure.

And, glory, the level garden
Will elevate the new
Perfection of its morning.

Now the heights are heavens,
Populous with light,
Without edge or penumbra.

The splendor springs again
As though a form akin
To its own hope indwelling.

Further: the flesh, in greater
Reality, ascends
Thus naked, unto fortune.

W. S. MERWIN

ESTACIÓN DEL NORTE

Pero la brutal baraúnda,
Esa muchedumbre que inunda
Nuestra común desolación . . .
Pero un andén se nos ofrece.
No creo en el número trece.
¡Potencia viva de estación!

Muchos viajamos. ¡Gran turismo!
Lejos no está ningún abismo.
—¿Cuál prefiere? —¿Yo? No, señor.
No quisiera más que una zona
Sin prohibición de persona
Ni obligaciones de temblor.

Esa angustia de una tiniebla
Que sólo de objetos se puebla . . .
Hombres han sido y todavía
Lo son porque sufren —de modo
Correcto a veces— bajo el lodo
Que enmascara aquella agonía.

GARE DU NORD

But this deafening brute uproar,
This rude stampede of men that pours
Upon our general desolation . . .
And onto a platform we are erupted.
Number Thirteen – but what do I care?
The power of life is held by this station!

The season for travel. Everyone on tour!
There's more than one hell nearby, be sure.
"And which do you prefer?" "Who, me?
None, thank you. I just want a place
Where a person isn't forced to debase
Himself, to cringe down on his knees."

How this gray twilight of dread
Seems populated only by objects . . .
These once were men and still are men
Because they suffer – in some cases
Even politely – behind clay faces
That mask the agony sealed within.

¿Tan turbia es nuestra incertidumbre
Que ni un rayo habrá que la alumbre?
El mundo se inclina a su muerte.
Hasta el silencio está roído
Por algún fantasma de ruido
Que en sordo abuso lo convierte.

¿Se empeña la Historia que diga
Toda voz a la dulce amiga
Que para salvar amenaza:
Quítame el peso de ser libre,
Déjame que sólo ya vibre
Con ilusión bajo tu maza?

Loquea en público el obseso,
Huyen bajo un odio confeso
Moribundos por los caminos.
Resplandecen los uniformes,
Crimen por ley, todos conformes,
Los aparatos son divinos.

Máquinas, máquinas... Y un humo
General: así me consumo.
¿Todo morirá en mala bruma?
No, no, no. Vencerá la Tierra,
Que en firmamento nos encierra:
Ya al magno equilibrio nos suma.

Is our perplexing anguish so dense
No ray of light can penetrate?
The world bows down to meet its death.
Even dear silence now is gnawed
By some phantasm of noise that makes
It change into a dumb abuse.

Is History required to tell
These freedom-lovers blatantly
That they must threaten in order to save:
"Take off this burden of being free,
Just let me go on living and be
Happy under your iron fist"?

The obsessed crassly exult in public,
And under a hatred that all admit,
Men facing death flee down the roads.
Uniforms shine resplendent;
With crime made legal, and all in consent,
The display is truly divine.

Machines, machines . . . The smoky gloom
Is everywhere, and I am consumed.
Will all perish in malignant fog?
No! Wrapping us in its firmament,
The Earth shall triumph: even now it adds
Us to its majestic harmony.

HUBERT CREEKMORE

MÁS VIDA

I

¿Por qué tú, por qué yo bajo el cielo admirable?
¿Por qué azar, por qué turno
De favor, por qué enlace
De laberinto, por qué gracia
De viaje
Prorrumpimos a ser, acertamos a estar
En el instante
Que se arrojaba hacia la maravilla?

Sí, salve.

II

Hijo, resplandor
De mi júbilo
Como el verso posible
Que busco.

Gracias a ti, figura de mi amor bajo el sol,
Restituído
Todo a esa luz y con alma visible a ti acudo,
Límpido.

MORE LIFE

I

Why you, why me, under this admirable sky?
By what hazard, by what turn
Of luck, by what passage
Of the labyrinth, by what grace
Of voyage
Do we burst into being and hit upon being now,
At the moment
That hurls itself forward toward marvels?

Yes, *salve*.

II

Son, brilliance
Of my joy
Like the possible poem
I look for.

Thanks to you, form of my love under the sun,
All that light is restored to me,
And with my soul made clear,
I turn myself to you.

En su interior el alma profundiza
Sin oscurecimiento.
Heme aquí de mi noche liberado,
Neto.

Hijo, ya impulso hacia la luz
Desde mi gozo:
Hay luz universal
Para tus ojos.

III

¡Cuántos siglos ahora sosteniéndote,
Y con su esfuerzo
Latentes, montañosos,
A tus pies emergiendo
Para levantar un futuro
Todavía tan leve y tan inquieto
Que apenas
Se insinúa en el aire de tu pecho!

IV

La mirada mía verá
Con tus ojos
El mejor universo:
El de tu asombro.

My soul goes deeply inside itself,
But without darkness.
Here I am freed of my night at last,
Purified.

Son, now started toward the light
From out of my desiring:
There is a universal light
For your eyes.

III

How many ages sustaining you now,
And with their force,
Latent, mountainous,
Emerging at your feet
To raise a future
At once so light and so turbulent
That it can hardly join
The air in your breathing chest!

IV

My sight will see
The best universe
Through your eyes:
That of your wonder.

A través de tus horas, sin descanso
Más allá de la muerte,
Hasta el año 2000 he de llegar
Calladamente.

Hijo tan asombrado, tan interior al círculo
Del enigma:
La Creación en creación
Es quien te sitia.

V

Hacia su plenitud
Mi mejor pensamiento,
Frente a mí se me planta,
Carne y hueso.
Eres.
     Y no soy libre.
¡Qué dulce así, ya prisionero
De mi vida más mía,
Ser responsable de tu aliento!
Tu realidad no deja escapatoria.
Eres mi término,
El término fatal de mi ternura.
¡Qué gozo en este apego
Sin ninguna razón,
En este celo
Tan obstinado tras la pequeñez!

Riding across your hours, without rest
On the other side of death,
I will have to arrive, in you,
At the year 2000, silently.

Son, so astonished, so inside the circle
Of the enigma,
Creation in creation
Is what besieges and surrounds you.

V

Toward its fulfillment
My best thought
Plants itself before me,
Flesh and bone.
You are.
          And I am not free.
How fine it is to be so, to be the prisoner
Of my own life made more mine in you,
To be responsible for your breath and spirit!
Your existence permits no escape.
You are my end,
The fated end result of my affections.
What joy in this attachment
With no reason at all,
In this so obstinate ardor
Toward what is small!

Profundo amor pequeño
Me fuerza
—Dentro de un orbe que es un cerco—
A gravitar, y así con mi vivir
Gravito, quiero,
Astro dichoso.
¡Oh dicha: preso!
                        Preso.
¿Quién eres, quién serás?
Existes. Eres. En tu mundo quedo.

VI

Hasta las raíces de mi orgullo profundiza,
Me cala,
Alto y ligero sobre el orgullo levantándome,
Tu gracia.

A tu gracia me rindo
Con mi poder.
Nada se puede contra el ángel.
El ángel es.

Entre las cosas y los sueños
Avanzas
Tan soñado, tan real que me descubro
Más cerca el alma.

Deep, small, particular love
Compels me –
Within a world that is a circle –
To gravitate, and thus with my whole life
I gravitate, I love
Highly, a fortunate star.
Ah, fortune: to be captive!

                                 Captive.
Who are you? Who will you be?
You exist. You are. I remain in your world.

VI

It goes right through me
Down to the roots of my pride,
And raises me up, light and high above pride:
Your grace.

I surrender to your grace
With all my forces.
Nothing can beat the angel.
The angel *is*.

You come on
Among dreams and real things,
So dreamed, so real, that I find
My own soul closer to me.

VII

Y tú,
Ya con el viento.
¡Qué desgarrón de claridad
En el silencio,
Cuánto espacio de luz esperanzada
En ese acecho
Que es el aire por Junio,
A la gracia dispuesto!
Y tú,
Ya con el viento.

VIII

Hijo, vislumbre
De gloria:
Cielos redondos ceñirán
Tus obras.

Cima apuntada hacia el azul escueto,
Sin celaje:
El amor mismo te dará
Sus valles.

No soy mi fin, no soy final
De vida.
Pase la corriente. No es tuya
Ni mía.

VII

And you,
Already off on the wind.
What a break-through of clarity
In the silence,
What a space of hoped-for light
In that ambush
Which is the air in June,
So well disposed toward grace!
And you,
Already off on the wind.

VIII

Son, glimpse
At glory,
Spherical heaven will surround
Your works.

A sharp peak pointed toward a blue faultless sky,
No trace of clouds:
True love itself
Will give you its valleys.

I am not my own ending, I am not
An ending of life.
Let the torrent go by. It is not yours
And not mine.

Hijo, centella
De un fuego:
En el gran fuego inextinguible
Quemémonos.

IX

Ardiendo pasa la corriente. ¡Salve!
Fuegos de creación
Siempre en nosotros, con nosotros arden

¿Llamas ocultas, de repente en alto,
Brincan, embisten, ágiles?

Errores con dolores,
Desastres.
¡Ay, luchas de Caín!

Y todo se deshace y se rehace.
¿Llamas y brasas?
Es el mundo invasor y de veras creándose,
Un mundo inmenso
De verdades,
Una inmensa verdad
De sangre.

Hijo:
Tu mundo, tu tesoro.

Son, spark
Of a fire:
In the great inextinguishable fire
Let us both burn.

IX

The current goes by, burning. *Salve!*
The fires of creation,
Always in us, with us burn.

O hidden flames, suddenly on high,
Do you leap up in combat, agilely?

Errors with dolors,
Disasters,
All the wars of Cain!

And everything unmakes and remakes itself.
Flames and living coals?
It is the invader world, and truly creating itself,
A huge world
Of truths,
A huge truth
Of blood.

Son:
Your world, your treasure.

ALAN DUGAN

MÁS ESPLENDOR

El calor ya:
Una temperatura de confianza en labios.
Presentimiento de calor hermoso
Promete espacios, lejanías claras,
Profundidad,
Profundidad que espera,
Profundidades con ternura.
Por ese resplandor
Una ternura flota disponible.

¡Aquí,
Tú misma!
Conmigo tú,
Profunda en el espacio soleado
Que te sostiene,
Cumbre de esperanza cumplida,
De inmediato secreto
Maravilloso.

Se asoma luz tangible al horizonte.
¡Cuántos valles detrás y cuántos aires
En torno de tu cuerpo,
Campo también, país y suma cándida!

GREATER MAGNIFICENCE

And the heat:
A temperature steady on lips.
An inkling of the heat's sweetness
Gives promise of space, shimmering expanses,
Deepness,
Deepness with hope in it,
Depths with gentleness.
Throughout that brilliance,
A gentleness floats about us.

You,
You here!
You with me,
Mysterious in the sun-filled space
Which bears you up,
The ultimate instance of hope fulfilled,
Of a secret, tangible,
Wonderful.

You can feel the light reaching to the horizon.
Deep valley and airs – so many! – hovering
About your body,
Fields, a whole country, a snowy wholeness!

Tú eres el día,
La ternura del día dominado,
La claridad en coto,
La poseída claridad
Bajo una profusión de sol difuso.
¡Y qué frescura de lejanía por tu cuerpo,
Claro cuerpo feliz
Como paisaje!
Tú misma, tú, callada y revelada,
Toda ofrecida a claridad en acto,
Máxima, férvida.

¡Oh continua, profunda suavidad de silencio!
La sangre corre.
¡Pleno vivir henchido de presente aceptado!
Todo es ahora.

Un asomo de vello apenas rubio.
Y se dora la piel como una fruta
Que se hiciese animal en nuestras manos,
El plumaje aun más tibio de sorpresa.
Nuca augural,
Hombros, rodillas, trabazones.
La exactitud es más ardiente.
¡Qué minucioso lujo de invención,
Cuánto oriente de pronto amaneciendo,
Rubio casi rosado
Con indicio de vena alboreada!

You are the day itself,
The softness of the day subdued,
Its clarity contained,
Its clarity held steady
Under a profusion of diffused sunlight.
And the cleanness of distances in your body,
Open, blessed,
Clear as a landscape!
You, you, in silence and yet revealed,
Offering all to the air's clearness,
Wholly, eagerly.

Let the silence flow on, smoothly, deeply!
The blood is flowing.
To live, brimming over with a present wholly
    accepted!
All is in now.

A trace of almost golden down.
Skin gilds over like fruit
Which turns to flesh in our hands,
Its aura warmed with surprise.
The promise of the nape,
Shoulders, knees, limbs.
The body is more exotic in its precision.
Luxurious its inventive intricacy,
This recognition suddenly dawning,
A gold almost gone pink,
The suspicion of a vein coming to light!

Y el país otra vez,
Cumbre, declive, curva en curso terso.
¿La pérdida en la carne inacabable?
Espaldas —y se olvidan.
¡Cuánta hermosura infiel a mi recuerdo,
Hermosura en aurora
Que no se aprende!

Ya se ciega el saber.
Enmudecen los gozos.
¡Gozos tendidos, gozos implorantes
Que tanto necesitan de su causa!
Labios y labios, labios
Con su querer, su gracia a solas,
Y para mí de pronto
Labios, tus labios,
Reales otra vez, soñados siempre:
Tan de veras lo son.

El alma se desliza por su cauce
Con gozo de caudal.
A través de este gozo, el mundo se despoja
De su desorden.

Quiero quererte,
Realidad de las Realidades.
¡Ah, vivir trasformado todo en rumbo!

And you become a country again,
A rise, a valley, a smooth, curving flow.
What is lost in the vagueness of flesh?
Shoulders – but one forgets them.
How unfaithful to beauty has been my
   remembering.
The dawning of sheer beauty
Beyond familiarity!

All that we know goes blind.
Sheer joy keeps its silence.
A joy so obvious, so eager –
What reason does it need!
Lips and lips, lips
With love in them, with their solitary grace,
And for me, suddenly
Lips, your lips
Grown real again, and always dreamed of;
So true they are.

The soul moves in its course
With the joy of abundance.
And through this joy, the world sloughs off
All its disorder.

All my wish is to love you,
The reality in Reality.
To live, transformed entirely as I go!

Me conduce el más dulce tesón inquisitivo.
Amor de tantos días se reconcentra ahora,
Todo actual, en un ímpetu, prórroga de
    relámpago.
¡Volver, siempre volver, querencia eterna!
Furia de fe nos lanza a vida y vida,
Más y más vida, sin temor de muerte.

¡Ah, ser eterno ya,
Sin dilación,
Todo en raíz
Trascender el impulso!

La armonía se cumple,
Total,
Deleite convertido en su ternura.
Gracias a ti yo existo, plenamente yo existo,
Gracias a ti, realísima,
En este instante que se cierra
Perfecto y para siempre.

¡Ser, ser,
Tesoro todo,
Extremo de sí mismo en esperanza,
Amor!
Y mientras, anhelar,
Anhelar con anhelo humilde
La gloria que se cumple,
Que sí se cumple ya absoluta,

A sweet persistence drives me.
Now my love of so many days gathers,
Actual, entire, sudden, a sustained lightning.
Always to return, return, this endless loving!
The fury of our faith hurls us from life to life,
More and more life, without a fear of dying.

Ah, this continuous being,
Undilating,
Deep in the root,
Beyond whim or impulse!

Harmony fulfills itself
Entirely,
Takes delight in its own gentleness.
By your grace I exist, I exist in my fullness.
By grace of you in all your reality,
In this single moment, now closed
Perfectly and forever.

Being, being,
Wealth entire,
And love,
Its own extreme of hoping!
And meanwhile, wanting,
Longing, with simple desire,
For the fulfilling glory
Now in fulfillment, absolutely,

Sin engaño absoluta para siempre:
La realidad en acto,
Angustiosa, gozosa, perfectísima.

Absolute, forever, undeceiving:
Reality in its happening,
Anxious, joyful, most miraculous.

ALASTAIR REID

NOCHE CÉNTRICA

Sobre suelos de estrella,
Con ardor fabulosas,
Noche y ciudad rielan.

En el asfalto fondos
De joyerías cándidas
Se aparecen a todos.

Letras de luz pronuncian,
Silabario del vértigo,
Palabrerías bruscas.

Las calles resplandecen.
Son óperas de incógnito.
Quisieran ser terrestres.

¡Óperas, sí, divinas,
Que se abren por las noches
En las estrellas vivas!

METROPOLITAN NIGHT

Above a surface of stars,
Night and the city, fabulous,
Shine with great heat.

Upon the asphalt, pale
Jewelry shops reveal
Their depths to all.

Letters of light pronounce –
Grammar of vertigo –
Their fretful rigmarole.

The glistening streets
Are acts of masquerade
That want to be part of earth.

Operas, yes, divine indeed;
Opening out through night
Upon the living stars!

BARBARA HOWES

PRESAGIO

Eres ya la fragancia de tu sino.
Tu vida no vivida, pura, late
Dentro de mí, tictac de ningún tiempo.

¡Qué importa que el ajeno sol no alumbre
Jamás estas figuras, sí, creadas,
Soñadas no, por nuestros dos orgullos!
        No importa. Son así más verdaderas
        Que el semblante de luces verosímiles
        En escorzos de azar y compromiso.

Toda tú convertida en tu presagio,
¡Oh, pero sin misterio! Te sostiene
La unidad invasora y absoluta.

¿Qué fue de aquella enorme, tan informe,
Pululación en negro de lo hondo,
Bajo las soledades estrelladas?
        Las estrellas insignes, las estrellas
        No miran nuestra noche sin arcanos.
        Muy tranquilo se está lo tan oscuro.

PORTENT

You are already the fragrance of your destiny.
Your unlived life, pure, beats
Within me, ticktock of no time.

What does it matter if the alien sun never
Illumines these shapes which, yes, are created,
Not dreamed, by our two prides!
   It does not matter. They are more true, thus,
   Than the appearance of plausible lights
   Foreshortened by hazard and compromise.

All of you transformed into your portent,
Oh, but without mystery! You are sustained
By the invading and absolute unity.

What became of that enormous, utterly formless
Budding in the black of the abyss
Under the starred solitudes?
   The celebrated stars, the stars
   Do not look upon our nights where nothing
    is hidden.
   There where it is so dark it is very calm.

La oscura eternidad ¡oh! no es un monstruo
Celeste. Nuestras almas invisibles
Conquistan su presencia entre las cosas.

Oh, the dark eternity is no celestial
Monster! Our invisible souls
Seize its presence in the midst of things.

W. S. MERWIN

QUIERO DORMIR

Más fuerte, más claro, más puro,
Seré quien fui.
Venga la dulce invasión del olvido.
Quiero dormir.

¡Si me olvidase de mí, si fuese un árbol
Tranquilo,
Ramas que tienden silencio,
Tronco benigno!

La gran oscuridad ya maternal,
Poco a poco profunda,
Cobije este cuerpo que al alma
—Una pausa— renuncia.

Salga ya del mundo infinito,
De sus accidentes,
Y al final del reposo estrellado
Seré el que amanece.

Abandonándome a la cómplice
Barca
Llegaré por mis ondas y nieblas
Al alba.

I WANT TO SLEEP

I shall be still stronger,
Still clearer, purer, so let
The sweet invasion of oblivion come on.
I want to sleep.

If I could forget myself, if I were only
A tranquil tree,
Branches to spread out the silence,
Trunk of mercy.

The great darkness, grown motherly,
Deepens little by little,
Brooding over this body that the soul –
After a pause – surrenders.

It may even embark from the endless world,
From its accidents,
And, scattering into stars at the last,
The soul will be daybreak.

Abandoning myself to my accomplice,
My boat,
I shall reach on my ripples and mists
Into the dawn.

No quiero soñar con fantasmas inútiles,
No quiero caverna.
Que el gran espacio sin luna
Me aísle y defienda.

Goce yo así de tanta armonía
Gracias a la ignorancia
De este ser tan seguro que se finge
Su nada.

Noche con su tiniebla, soledad con su paz,
Todo favorece
Mi delicia de anulación
Inminente.

¡Anulación, oh paraíso
Murmurado,
Dormir, dormir y sólo ser
Y muy despacio!

Oscuréceme y bórrame,
Santo sueño,
Mientras me guarda y vela bajo su potestad
El firmamento.

Con sus gravitaciones más umbrías
Reténgame la tierra,
Húndase mi ser en mi ser:
Duerma, duerma.

I do not want to dream of useless phantoms,
I do not want a cave.
Let the huge moonless spaces
Hold me apart, and defend me.

Let me enjoy so much harmony
Thanks to the ignorance
Of this being, that is so secure
It pretends to be nothing.

Night with its darkness, solitude with its peace,
Everything favors
My delight in the emptiness
That soon will come.

Emptiness, O paradise
Rumored about so long:
Sleeping, sleeping, growing alone
Very slowly.

Darken me, erase me,
Blessed sleep,
As I lie under a heaven that mounts
Its guard over me.

Earth, with your darker burdens,
Drag me back down,
Sink my being into my being:
Sleep, sleep.

JAMES WRIGHT

V

WHOLENESS OF BEING

Who has ever gloried in fortune
But might say to himself . . .

CALDERÓN

MUNDO EN CLARO

Eres tú quien florece y resucita.

ANTONIO MACHADO

I

¡Ah!
    De pronto, sin querer,
Heme aquí. ¡No soy fantasma!
Hallándome voy en una
Vaguedad que se declara,
Una especie de indolencia
Donde estoy. ¡Yo! Pulpa cálida
A oscuras se apelotona.
Del silencio se levantan
Murmullos: silencio . . . mío.
Entre nieblas, entre sábanas
Permanece elemental
Una convicción. Se entraña
Mi ser en mi ser. Yo soy.
Yo, yo: somnolencia grata.
¡Cuánta dulzura en seguir,
En perseverar! El alma,
Veladora, siempre erguida
Sobre el sueño, me acompaña
Sin presentarse a través
De mi olvido. ¡Bien!
                    Lejana

MANIFEST WORLD

> It is you who bloom and revive.
>
> ANTONIO MACHADO

I

Ah!
  Suddenly, not wishing to,
I am there! No chimera —
I encounter myself and move
Through a haze that unfolds
In an image of torpor that attends me
Wherever I am. The temperate pulp that is I
Obscurely englobes itself;
The silence is stirred —
Murmurs: a silence . . . my own.
Between cloud wrack, bedded down in our linens,
Elemental conviction
Remains. My being
Is pierced with my being. I am!
Myself, I myself: a blessed quiescence.
How good the unwearied travail,
The pursuit! That keeper of vigils,
The soul erect in its station, unceasingly
Poised on our dreaming, moves with me here
Through whatever it is I forget,
And will not declare itself. It is well.

         Far from us,

Bajo el último sopor
Aun lejano, la mirada
Columbra, recuerda. ¡Bulto
Soñoliento! Sí, descansa,
Como siempre. Perfección
De la vida cotidiana:
Aquí estás. Sin voluntad,
Yacente —de tan salvada,
Abandonas tu candor
Indefenso a la campaña
Nocturna de las estrellas,
Pendientes sobre la almohada.
Estas horas que no saben
De tu dormir, solitarias,
Mas tan dulcemente adictas
A tu reposo, te alzan
A un nivel tan serenado,
Tan firme, de tal bonanza
Que entre lo oscuro y las cosas
Pone amor.
                    Y se congracia
La respiración —hay paz
Tuya en la noche estrellada—
Con el latido del orbe,
A quien sin embargo alcanza
La soledad vigilante,
Pacificadora, sabia.
Tu pulso, mientras, insiste,
A los astros acompasa.

In an ultimate lethargy
No less remote to us, the source of all gazing
Recalls and distinguishes. O brooding
Configurement! Rest,
Now as at all times.
O daily perfection of things,
You are here. Not willing it,
You lie fallow – so sure in your probity
You yield yourself up on the starry
Plateaus of the night
Overhanging this pillow.
The hours, knowing nothing at all
Of your slumber, alone under heaven,
The solicitous wards
Of your sleeping, now bear you aloft
Into perfect serenity,
The poise whose abundance
Fixes, between what is dark and the things
Of this world, the shape of our love.

                                       Our breathing
Delights us – the peace
That is wrought on a night full of stars
Is yours – with the planet's pulsation,
Where mounts, at all hazard,
Assuaging and watchful and wise,
The genius of solitude.
And the throb of your pulses persist
To apportion the stars in that interval.

Por las sienes, por el pecho
De continuo palpitada,
Una paciencia animal
Se infunde en lo oscuro. ¡Calma!
Al corazón no le oigo.
Pero toda mi esperanza
Cae bajo el poderío
De ese tictac, que no para
De fundir lo más real
Con su compás, con su magia.
¡Sueño activo, qué de estrellas
Siempre en torno desveladas!

II

Lo oscuro pierde espesor.
Triunfa el cristal. La ventana
Va ensanchando hasta el confín
Posible la madrugada,
Flotante en una indolencia
Que no es mía. Todo vaga.
Una indecisión de nube
Forma un conato de estancia.
Entre jirones de muebles,
A los espejos aguardan
Los volúmenes confusos:
Caos dentro de una casa,
Pero con mucha inocencia

Through brow and through breast
The unwearying beat
Of an animal patience
Flows in on the darkness. Peace!
Not with a heartbeat I hear you —
But all expectation
Surrenders itself to the might
Of that ticktock, the unceasing
Convergence of things as they are
In the magic and scope of the actual.
O strenuous dream, eternally ringed
In the vigilant circling of stars!

II

Dark loses its density.
Window glass flourishes. The windowpane
Widens its margins, enlarges its compass
In the total extension of morning,
Drifts in an indolence
Not of my making. Shadowy, shadowy.
A cloud's hesitations
Shape the guess of a human interior:
Between tatterdemalion furniture,
Indeterminate bulk
Waits for a looking glass:
The chaos that lives inside houses —
But in infinite innocence

Caótica.
　　　¡Leve el alba!
Aunque gravite con fe,
—La fe en un mundo de gracia,
Regalado— todo pesa
Ligeramente. Ya baja
La luz a señorear
Hasta las sombras dejadas
A los sueños. No hay ventura
Mayor que esta concordancia
Del ser con el ser. Ahora
Ni alumbra gozo. ¡Se arraiga
La vida con tal raíz
Dentro de su necesaria
Profundidad! Sin cesar
Asombra la simple marcha
Del tiempo, de este minuto
Que por el presente pasa
Resonando, fácil. Es
La incógnita soberana.
¡Tictac!
　　　¡Tictac! Y comienzas
A sentir la mescolanza
De mi vigilia y tu fondo
Grave. ¿Duermes? ¡Cómo enlazas
Y remontas el borrón
De esa intemperie a la talla
De este concierto final
Que a los dormidos ampara!

Chaotic!
       Then, daybreak!
However that faith presses in on us –
Faith in the grace of a world
Gratuitously given – all weighs on us
Lightly. Now, overmastering all,
Probing the darkness we keep in our dreaming,
Brightness moves down on the air. What enterprise
Greater than this – the kinship of Being
With a being! For even
Delight does not dazzle. Life roots itself
Down with a thread that transfixes
Essential profundity. Unceasing,
The simple progressions of time
Display themselves, from a moment of being
That glides through time present
And resonates freely. The sovereign
Incognito –
Ticktock!
       Ticktock! You are stirred
By a medley that merges my vigil
With your somber profundity.
Do you sleep still? How you twine
And replenish the blur
Of a climate's inconstancy, to the shape
Of a final accord
That shelters all sleepers!
Do you sleep, then? The blazons of memory
Break into view on the mask

¿Duermes? Memoria en relieve
Va aflorando por la máscara
De soñar, que poco a poco
Se va convirtiendo en cara.
¿No están ya los entresueños
Enredándose en la trama
De grises, blancos y azules
Que por la atmósfera llaman?
Quiebra el albor.
              Y la aurora
Difunde una llamarada.
Amarilla se deslíe
Por entre el carmín y el grana.
Con resplandor y rumor,
Invasores, avasalla
Siempre el día. ¡Qué temprano
Suena a calles estrenadas
Otra vez! Vuelve a vivir,
A esperar la luz humana,
Enamoradiza ya
Por balcones y fachadas.

III

Y en un arranque, por fin,
—Beata elección, beata
Querencia— tiendes los brazos.
Es de verdad la mañana

Of your dreaming: little by little,
It alters itself to a face.
Are those dreams-in-between-dreams still
Weaving themselves in the web
Of the fabric – the grays and the whites and the
    blues
That call through the ether?
Daybreak.
                The dawn
Sends out scintillations.
Yellow unpacks itself
Between carmine and scarlet,
Conquistadors, splendid
And resonant; day
Is forever subdued. How early it stirs
On the thoroughfares, trying existence
Again! And lives again, here,
Awaiting a human transparence
Whose love dwells adoringly now
Upon balconies, porches, façades of a city.

III

In the flash of an impulse, at last –
O blessed predilection, blessèd
Solicitude! – you hold out your arms.
The truth of the day's consummation

Que se cumple, que termina
De amanecer, entregada.
Así, con exactitud
De cuerpos celestes, hacia
Mí tus brazos ya solares
Se dirigen.
        Y la fábrica
De nuestro día en el centro
De la claridad resalta.
El caos fue, no será.
A todos nos arrebata
Con su fuerza de invasión,
De maravilla esta máquina
Del mundo. ¡Sin maravilla
Mínima no apunta nada!
Cierto: llega a ser discreta.
Follajes hay que resguardan
Por entre el ruido y el fárrago
Silenciosas enramadas.
Todavía en el silencio
Perduran nuestras palabras
De mayor fe. ¿Las adviertes
Bajo el ímpetu del ansia
Por amar, cantar, saltar?
Ante la clara jornada
Tan vivo está lo vivido
Que al futuro se abalanza.
Y con abandono apenas
Iluminado —pestañas

Is here: dawn closes its changes
And surrenders itself without quarter.
So, with a planet's
Exactitude, your arms, made celestial
And solar, turn to me.
                              And the mesh
Of our day rebounds with a start
In the center of clarity.
The chaos that was, will not be!
Miraculously, now, the machine
Of the world, like a breaching of armies,
Strikes home to us fully,
And sweeps us before it. For, lacking the touch
Of the marvelous, nothing is notable.
True, it takes on a reticence:
There are coverts that hold in their leafage
Between din and dishevelment
All the verdure of silence.
And in silence, the speech
Of all that is best in our troth
Lives on for us, always. Under
The surge of that longing
To break into singing, to leap up in air,
To love – do you mark it?
Beyond our bright day span,
How hotly the animate flashes
And hurls itself into futurity!
And with what grazingly brightened
Abandon – O hazardous

Perezosas que no barren
Su penumbra rezagada—
El abrazo nuevamente
Gozoso al mundo nos ata.
¿No adivinas entre círculos
Favorables las distancias?
Todo un mundo redondea
Con sus cielos y sus ráfagas
Este refugio de sol
Íntimo, que no se apaga
Nunca para nuestros ojos.
¡Claridades entrañadas!
Sólo amor responde a mundo.
Aunque afine su maraña,
No luce el mal. ¡Laberinto
De callejas! Mundo es plaza:
Plaza con sol donde el viento,
Soleado, se remansa.
¡De día!
              Vuelve a su luz
Inmortal, a esta diaria
Tensión de amor el prodigio
Del mundo. Amor: escala,
Única tal vez, a vida
Sin término —si no engaña
La promesa irresistible
De tanta luz aliada
Cuando los brazos se juntan
En una gloria inmediata.

Eyelashes that do not occlude
Their reluctant penumbra –
The embrace, as if never
Delighting before, binds us fast to the world.
Can you trace, in that happy
Encircling, the distances?
The whole of a world, with its
Skies and its flashings of lusters,
Arches a refuge of intimate
Sun that never will lessen
Its flame, to our gaze.
Transparencies, pure to the quick!
How answer a world, save by love?
However it tighten its skeins,
Evil goes lightless. O maze
On the alleyways! The world is our thoroughfare:
Plazas in sunlight, where the wind
In a burnish of sunlight rides on the eddies.
All's daylight!
                    The prodigal world
Comes back in perpetual light
To habitual tensions, to the stress
Of its loving. O Love! We mount by a stairway
No less unmatchable, into life
Without end – if the pledges,
Invincible now, do not cozen us –
There where all radiance joins
And our arms have encircled to touch
Instantaneous glory.

                                   BEN BELITT

MUCHACHAS

Presentando la colina
Se esparce una mocedad
—Más rubia en su regocijo—
Que se escapa, que se va
Por entre un verdor y un sol
De fuentes.
              ¡Fuentes! Atrás
Vencido en figura un fresno,
Se asoma a una intimidad
De prado en flor sorprendida
La más Esbelta.
              ¿La más
Esbelta?
              Brotan, se alzan
—Bucles hacia su espiral
Y melenas sobre cuellos
Erguidos con un afán
De tallo aún— creaciones
De Primer Jardín.
              Está
Culminando, fascinando
—Iris de su manantial—
Ese impulso hacia la fábula
Que es de un dios y es realidad.

YOUNG GIRLS

Coming in view on the hill
Young people are making merry –
Pink cheeks reflecting their joy –
Then make good their escape, run off
To enter a green world and fountains
Of sunlight.
     Fountains! Far off,
Against a stand of ash trees –
Surpassing them – one sees
The shapliest appear,
In friendship with that field
Of surprised flowers.
       The
Shapliest?
    They burst forth, they stand erect –
Curls in their spirals,
Locks flowing free over necks
Like shoots eager
To aspire further – creations
Of Eden's garden.
      All is
Reaching its height, enchanting –
A very rainbow in its flowing –
This impulse toward legend
Issues from a god and is reality.

BARBARA HOWES

LAS DOCE EN EL RELOJ

Dije: ¡Todo ya pleno!
Un álamo vibró.
Las hojas plateadas
Sonaron con amor.
Los verdes eran grises,
El amor era sol.
Entonces, mediodía,
Un pájaro sumió
Su cantar en el viento
Con tal adoración
Que se sintió cantada
Bajo el viento la flor
Crecida entre las mieses,
Más altas. Era yo,
Centro en aquel instante
De tanto alrededor,
Quien lo veía todo
Completo para un dios.
Dije: Todo, completo.
¡Las doce en el reloj!

TWELVE O'CLOCK

I declared: Everything in fullness now!
A lone poplar stirred,
Its silvery leaves
Sounding with love.
The greens were grays,
The love was sunlight.
And then, noonday,
A bird immersed
His song in the wind
With such adoration
That beneath the winds
The flower felt itself sung,
Growing among the tallest
Grain. It was I,
At that moment center
Of so much surrounding,
Who saw everything
Complete for a god.
There it is, I said, complete.
It was twelve o'clock!

NORMAN THOMAS DI GIOVANNI

239

ARDOR

Ardor. Cornetines suenan,
Tercos, y en las sombras chispas
Estallan. Huele a un metal
Envolvente. Moles. Vibran
Extramuros despoblados
En torno a casas henchidas
De reclusión y de siesta.
En sí la luz se encarniza.
¿Para quién el sol? Se juntan
Los sueños de las avispas.
¿Quedará el ardor a solas
Con la tarde? Paz vacía,
Cielo abandonado al cielo,
Sin un testigo, sin línea.
Pero sobre un redondel
Cae de repente y se fija,
Redonda, compacta, muda,
La expectación. Ni respira.
¡Qué despejado lo azul,
Qué gravitación tranquila!
Y en el silencio se cierne
La unanimidad del día,
Que ante el toro estupefacto

ARDOR

Ardently. Cornets with an adamant
Sound that explodes in a shadowy
Flashing of tinders. That smell,
Like a meeting of metals. Densities. Beyond,
Where the houses lie gorged with their solitude,
In the noon of their torpor, bereft of the living,
All goes to distance, and trembles.
There the light lives enraged.
Whom would the sun serve? The dreaming
Of wasps is joined in a common vagary.
Shall the ardors persist in their singlehood
Into the evening? A vacant serenity:
Sky left alone with the sky,
Unscored by a line, unbeholdable.
Yet in the circle,
Mute and compact in its round,
Expectancy startles us, striking down
And implanting itself. Not so much
As a breath! How fleckless the reaches of blue:
O serene gravitation!
And now in the silence sifts down
All the day's unanimity
That centers its yellows and gathers

Se reconcentra amarilla.
Ardor: reconcentración
De espíritus en sus dichas.
Bajo Agosto van los seres
Profundizándose en minas.
¡Calientes minas del ser,
Calientes de ser! Se ahincan,
Se obstinan profundamente
Masas en bloques. ¡Canícula
De bloques iluminados,
Plenarios, para más vida!
—Todo en el ardor va a ser,
Amor, lo que más sería.
¡Ser más, ser lo más y ahora,
Alzarme a la maravilla
Tan mía, que está aquí ya,
Que me rige! La luz guía.

Its force for the bull's stupefaction.
Ardors: the spirit has fixed itself fast
In its vantage and recentered its being.
The living move under August
Augmenting their selfhoods, deepening self
Like a mine. The hot mines of being,
The blazing of being! Intact in the block,
The masses implant themselves
And contrive their totality.
The radiant block of the dog days,
Plenitudes, making life more!
— Beloved, all things that live in their ardors
Shall inherit their perfect requital.
To be more! To be perfect in being, awake
In the wonderment, to be wholly
My own in the wonder that goes with me here,
Overmastering me! See: the light leads.

BEN BELITT

LA SALIDA

¡Salir por fin, salir
A glorias, a rocíos,
—Certera ya la espera,
Ya fatales los ímpetus—
Resbalar sobre el fresco
Dorado del estío
—¡Gracias!— hasta oponer
A las ondas el tino
Gozoso de los músculos
Súbitos del instinto,
Lanzar, lanzar sin miedo
Los lujos y los gritos
A través de la aurora
Central de un paraíso,
Ahogarse en plenitud
Y renacer clarísimo,
—Rachas de espacios vírgenes,
Acordes inauditos—
Feliz, veloz, astral,
Ligero y sin amigo!

GOING OUT

To go out! To take off at last
For glories, for new dewfalls —
The waiting come to a head,
The impulse become inevitable —
To glide out over the fresh
Gilding of summer —
Thanks! — and then to fight
The waves with the fine
Tone of the muscles,
Immediate with instinct,
To go out, to launch without fear
All extravagances and cries
Across a dawn
At the heart of a paradise!
To be drowned in fullness,
To be reborn extremely clear —
Fair winds from virgin spaces,
Unheard-of correspondences —
To be happy, fast, high,
Buoyant and absolutely alone!

ALAN DUGAN

ARENA

Retumbos. La resaca
Se desgarra en crujidos
Pedregosos. Retumbos.
Un retroceso arisco
Se derrumba, se arrastra.
¡Molicie en quiebra, guijos
En pedrea, tesón
En contra! De improviso,
¡Alto!
    ¿Paz?
        Y una ola
Pequeña cae sin ruido
Sobre la arena, suave
De silencio. ¡Qué alivio,
Qué sosiego! ¡Silencio
De siempre, siempre antiguo!
Porque Dios, sin edad,
Tiene ante sí los siglos.
Sobre la arena duran
Calladamente limpios.
Retumbe el mar, no importa.
¡El silencio allí mismo!

THE SAND

Booming! Then the surf
Withdraws, clattering
With rocks. Booming:
Then a fierce withdrawal.
It comes in like an avalanche,
Then drags itself out.
Frangibles in breakage! Stones
In lapidation! Tenacities
Opposed! Then, suddenly,
A halt!
      Peace?
            And a small wave
Falls noiselessly
Over the sand: gently,
In silence. What a comfort!
How calming! The silence
Of forever, forever old!
Because God, being ageless,
Has the ages before him.
Their silenced limpidities
Perdure over the sands.
The sea roars, but don't worry:
The silence is always there!

ALAN DUGAN

247

INVOCACIÓN

Sabes callar. Me sonríe,
Amor, desnuda tu boca.

Una espera —como un alma
Que desenvuelve su forma—
Sobre los labios ondula,
Se determina, se aploma.
    Yo quiero profundizar,
    Profundizar —imperiosa,
    Encarnizada ternura—
    En tu frescor, en sus conchas.

Con el beso, bajo el beso
Te busco, te imploro toda,
Esencial, feliz, desnuda,
Radiante, consoladora.
    Consuelo hasta el más recóndito
    Desamparo de la sombra,
    Consuelo por plenitud
    Que a la eternidad afronta.

Sabes callar. Me sonríe,
Amor, desnuda tu boca.

INVOCATION

Be silent. Smile at me,
Love, with your naked mouth.

Waiting – as a soul
Unfolding its own shape –
Hovers over the lips,
Decides, and falls away.
       I desire to fathom,
       Fathom again – a proud,
       Inflaming tenderness –
       There in your coolness, in your spiraling
          ways.

With a kiss, below the kiss,
You I seek, and I beg all of you,
Basic, perfect, naked,
Radiant, comforting.
       O joy, even to the utmost hidden
       Abandonment of the spirit,
       Joy through a fullness
       That looks eternity in the face.

Be silent. Smile at me,
Love, with your naked mouth.

BARBARA HOWES

ESTA LUNA

¡La luna!

        Cuando descubres
Los contornos de lo oscuro,
Hasta la sombra sin nombre
Queda amiga junto al curso
De tu fulgor familiar.
No, no serás el refugio
Que de los cielos resurge
Para el lacrimoso iluso.
Tranquilamente prosigues
Iluminando tu rumbo.
¿Quién revela más desnuda
Su verdad que tú, rotundo
Rostro? Con una sonrisa
Firme, contemplando a muchos
Frente a frente, presidiendo
Redondeas tu nocturno
Señorío. Para todos
Eres el portento justo,
Colmado de aparición
Dulcísima.

        ¡Plenilunio!

THIS MOON

Moon!

    When you approach
The edges of darkness
Even the nameless shadow
Is friendly near the course
Of your simple light.
Never will you be a refuge
Rising from heaven
For sorrowing dreamers.
You proceed without fanfare
To light up your own way.
Round face, who reveals
His truth more nakedly
Than you? With a firm smile,
Beholding mankind
Face to face, presiding,
You round out your nocturnal
Domain. For everyone
You are the perfect portent,
A presence brimmed with
Sweetness.

    Full moon!

MARK STRAND

EL AIRE

Aire: nada, casi nada,
O con un ser muy secreto,
O sin materia tal vez,
Nada, casi nada: cielo.

Con sigilo se difunde.
Nadie puede ver su cuerpo.
He ahí su misma Idea.
Aire claro, buen silencio.

Hasta el espíritu el aire,
Que es ya brisa, va ascendiendo
Mientras una claridad
Traspasa la brisa al vuelo.

Un frescor de trasparencia
Se desliza como un témpano
De luz que fuese cristal
Adelgazándose en céfiro.

¡Qué celeste levedad,
Un aire apenas terreno,
Apenas una blancura
Donde lo más puro es cierto!

THE AIR

Air: nothing, almost nothing,
Or else with an essence kept secret,
Or with perhaps no real substance,
Nothing, almost nothing: sky.

It spreads out in silent ways.
No one can see its body.
Look! It is the Idea of itself.
Clear air, sweet soundlessness.

Air now a current
Climbs to the realm of spirit,
And in its flight as a soft wind
It is pierced with brilliancy.

The cool transparent air
Glides like an ice floe
Of light – was it crystal once? –
Then tapers to a gentle breeze.

What celestial buoyancy!
Air hardly of this earth,
Hardly a trace of white
Even where purity is certain.

Aire noble que se otorga
Distancias, alejamientos.
Ocultando su belleza
No quiere parecer nuevo.

Aire que respiro a fondo,
De muchos soles muy denso,
Para mi avidez actual
Aire en que respiro tiempo.

Aquellos días de entonces
Vagan ahora disueltos
En este esplendor que impulsa
Lo más leve hacia lo eterno.

Muros ya cerca del campo
Guardan ocres con reflejos
De tardes enternecidas
En los altos del recuerdo.

¡Cómo yerra por la atmósfera
Su dulzura conduciendo
Los pasos y las palabras
Adonde van sin saberlo!

Algo cristalino en vías
Quizá de enamoramiento
Busca en un aura dorada
Sendas para el embeleso.

The noble air delineates
Perspectives, distances,
But not wishing to seem novel
Conceals its own beauty.

Air that I breathe deeply,
Dense with so many past suns.
For my present hunger,
Air in which I breathe time.

Those days of other years
Hover now, dissolved
In this radiance which urges
The lightest things toward the eternal.

On the heights of memory,
Walls at the edge of the country
Still hold their ochers in the reflected light
Of tender afternoons.

How their sweetness wanders
Through the atmosphere, leading
My footsteps and words
To where they stray without knowing it!

Crystalline air, perhaps
On roads to love,
Seeks in a golden breeze
The way to delight.

Respirando, respirando
Tanto a mis anchas entiendo
Que gozo del paraíso
Más embriagador: el nuestro.

Y la vida, sin cesar
Humildemente valiendo,
Callada va por el aire,
Es aire, simple portento.

Vida, vida, nada más
Este soplo que da aliento,
Aliento con una fe:
Sí, lo extraordinario es esto.

Esto: la luz en el aire,
Y con el aire un anhelo.
¡Anhelo de trasparencia,
Sumo bien! Respiro, creo.

Más allá del soliloquio,
Todo mi amor dirigiendo
Se abalanzan los balcones
Al aire del universo.

¡Balcones como vigías
Hasta de los más extremos
Puntos que la tarde ofrece
Posibles, amarillentos!

Breathing, breathing
As freely as I like, I know
I possess the most intoxicating
Of all paradises: our own.

And life, its humble worth
Never ceasing,
Moves silently through the air,
Indeed *is* air, a simple wonder.

This breath of air that gives us being,
Being with promise, is life,
Life itself and nothing else.
Yes, the extraordinary thing is this.

This: the light held in the air,
And with the air a longing.
Longing for pure transparency,
The highest good! I breathe, I believe.

Beyond soliloquy,
Balconies are thrown open
Directing all my love
To the air of the universe.

Balconies like watchtowers
As far as the utmost
Possible points – all turning yellow –
Which the afternoon bestows!

Mis ojos van abarcando
La ordenación de lo inmenso.
Me la entrega el panorama,
Profundo cristal de espejo.

Entre el chopo y la ribera,
Entre el río y el remero
Sirve, transición de gris,
Un aire que nunca es término.

¡Márgenes de la hermosura!
A través de su despejo,
El tropel de pormenores
No es tropel. ¡Qué bien sujeto!

Profundizando en el aire
No están solos, están dentro
Los jardinillos, las verjas,
Las esquinas, los aleros . . .

En el contorno del límite
Se complacen los objetos,
Y su propia desnudez
Los redondea: son ellos.

¡Islote primaveral,
Tan verdes los grises! Fresnos,
Aguzando sus ramillas,
Tienden un aire más tierno.

More and more my eyes embrace
The order of the infinite,
Surrendered up to me by the panorama
Like some deep crystal looking glass.

Between river and oarsman,
Between poplar and shore,
There hangs, a transition of gray,
An air which is always a passage.

Margins of beauty!
Through their sharp clarity
The confusion of details
Is not confusion. It is well composed!

Deepening in the air,
Nothing stands alone: the tiny gardens,
The grilled windows, the corners
And eaves are submerged in air.

In the sharpness of their edges
Objects seem to take delight,
And their own nakedness
Fills them out: they are what they are.

A stand of trees in springtime,
How green the grays! Ashes,
Urging leaves along their twigs,
Offer a more tender air.

El soto. La fronda. Límpidos,
Son esos huecos aéreos
Quienes mejor me serenan,
Si a contemplarlos acierto.

Feliz el afán, se colma
La tensión de un día pleno.
Volúmenes de follajes
Alzan un solo sosiego.

Torres se doran amigas
De las mieses y los cerros,
Y entre la luz y las piedras
Hay retozos de aleteos.

En bandadas remontándose
Juegan los pájaros. Vedlos.
Todos van, retornan, giran,
Contribuyen al gran juego.

¡Juego tal vez de una fuerza
No muy solemne, tanteo
De formas que sí consiguen
La perfección del momento!

Esta perfección, tan viva
Que se extiende al centelleo
Más distante, me presenta
Como una red cuanto espero.

The grove. The foliage. Aloft
Those limpid openings
Are what best grant me serenity
If I contemplate them well.

My efforts are lucky, the strain
Of a day replete brims over.
The volumes of leafage
Erect a single repose.

In the golden light, stone towers are friends
Of the wheat fields and the hills,
And from that vast radiance and the stones
Comes a frolic of fluttering.

Swifts are at play
In soaring flocks. Look at them:
Wheeling, tumbling, sailing,
All joining in the great game.

The game of a not very solemn
Power perhaps, a testing
Of forms that really do attain
The perfection of the moment.

And this perfection, so alive
It reaches to the remotest
Scintillation, presents to me
As in a net everything I hope for.

¡Aquel desgarrón de sol!
Arden nubes y no lejos.
Mientras, sin saber por qué,
Se ilumina mi deseo.

Arbolados horizontes
—Verdor imperecedero—
Dan sus cimas al dominio
Celeste, gloria en efecto.

Gloria de blancos y azules
Purísimos, violentos,
Algazaras de celajes
Que anuncian dioses y fuegos.

La realidad, por de pronto,
Sobrepasa anuncio y sueño
Bajo el aire, por el aire
Ceñido de firmamento.

El aire claro es quien sueña
Mejor. ¡Solar de misterio!
Con su creación el aire
Me cerca. ¡Divino cerco!

A una creación continua
—Soy del aire— me someto.
¡Aire en trasparencia! Sea
Su señorío supremo.

That gaping hole of sunlight!
Clouds are burning, and not far off.
Meanwhile, without my knowing why,
My own desire is filled with light.

Wooded horizons –
Evergreen forests –
Submit their peaks to the dominion
Of the heavens, in fact, to glory.

Glory of whites and blues,
The purest, the most intense:
Joyous clamor of wind-driven clouds
Proclaiming gods and fires.

Reality by now
Surpasses prophecy and dream,
Beneath the air, through the air
Wedded to the firmament.

It is clear air which best
Dreams. Mansion of mystery!
With its creation the air
Encircles me. O divine enclosure!

To a continuous creation –
For I am of air – I surrender myself.
Air in translucency! Let
Its sovereign power be supreme!

HUBERT CREEKMORE

CARA A CARA

Lo demás es lo otro: viento triste,
Mientras las hojas huyen en bandadas.

FEDERICO GARCIA LORCA

I

Verde oscuro amarillento,
Deslumbra un tigre. Fosfórico,
El círculo de agresión
General cierra su coso.

    Aun los cielos se barajan
    —Múltiples, bárbaros, lóbregos—
    Para formar una sola
    Sombra de dominio a plomo.

Nublado. Las nubes sitian
A las torres y cimborrios
De la ciudad, de improviso
Campestre. Se aguza un chopo
Bajo un retumbo que lejos
Se extingue, derrumbe sordo.
En el aire cruelmente
Blando se ahuman los troncos,
Y un crepúsculo a deshora
Derrama en el día golfos
De una oscuridad que pide
Luz urgente de socorro.

FACE TO FACE

The rest happens otherwise: a sad wind
While the leaves scatter in flurries.

I

Dark green gone to yellow,
A tiger has dazzled us. Phosphorescent,
The circuit of common assault
Shuts its arena.

Even the heavens entangle –
Multiple, sullen, and barbarous –
To shape to a plumb line the desolate
Shades of dominion.

Cloudily. Clouds now encompass
The towers and domes
Of the city, unforeseeably
Countrified. A poplar sharpens its edges
Under a clamor that fails
On the distance, a deaf downfall.
In that pitiless softness of air
The tree trunks go smoky,
Twilight unseasonably
Sheds on the day the abysses
Of darkness that ask
Only light's ardor to succor them.

Se encienden lámparas íntimas
Que recogen en sus conos
De resplandor esos ámbitos
Amigos de los coloquios.

Hay una desolación
A contra luz, algo anónimo
Que zumba hostil, un difuso
Conflicto de tarde y lodo
—Con su tedio, que no deja
De escarbar. Y de sus hoyos
Emergen desparramándose,
Asfixiando, los enojos
Escondidos, la más fosca
Pululación del bochorno,
El hervidero enemigo
De cuantos dioses invoco.

En relámpagos se rasgan
Los cielos hasta esos fondos
Tan vacíos que iluminan
Los cárdenos dolorosos.

El agresor general
Va rodeándolo todo.
—Pues . . . aquí estoy. Yo no cedo.
Nada cederé al demonio.

The lamps kindle, intimate:
They gather again in their cones
All that compass of brightness
That companions our causeries.

'Yet athwart all that light
Desolation remains, something nameless
That hums at us to our harm, the inchoate
Encounter of dusk and the bog –
The boredom that grows and will grant us
No respite. And out of the barrows
Emerge all the hidden malignities
Loosing themselves on the air, stopping our
    breathing,
The sinister swarms of our blood heat,
An inimical boiling and bubbling
Of the numberless gods we invoke.

In that lightning, the order of heaven
Is rent to its uttermost depths
And lights for us, out of its emptiness,
What is heartsick and dark in ourselves.

Our common antagonist goes binding
All things in his circuit. But –
I stand firm in this place. I do not make over.
I yield nothing at all to the demon.

II

¡Oh doliente muchedumbre
De errores con sus agobios
Innúmeros! Ved. Se asoman,
Míos también, a mi rostro.

Equivalencia final
De los unos y los otros:
Esos cómplices enlaces
De las víctimas y el ogro,

Mientras con su pesadumbre
De masa pesan los lomos
Reunidos del país
Polvoriento, populoso . . .

Las farsas, las violencias,
Las políticas, los morros
Húmedos del animal
Cínicamente velloso,

Y la confabulación
Que envuelve en el mismo rojo
De una iracundia común
Al paladín con el monstruo . . .

II

O suffering multitude,
Caught in your errors' unending
Repining! Only look! How they declare
   themselves –
My own with the others – here in my face!

That conclusive equivalence
Of the one and the many:
Those enlacing accomplices
Of victim and ogre,

While with the bulk of their
Heaviness their backs are borne downward,
Reassembled again from a populous
And powdery country . . .

Farces and bloodlettings,
Political gambits, the dampening
Snouts of the animal
Cynically shagged with a down,

And the shifts of collusion
That enmesh, in a common
Resentment's identical reds,
Crusader and monster . . .

Esa congoja del alba
Que blanquea el calabozo,
Extenuación de la cal
Sobre los muros monótonos,

A la vista siempre el aire
Tan ancho tras los cerrojos,
Y en la boca —siempre seca—
Tan amargo el soliloquio . . .

Ese instante de fatiga
Que sueña con el reposo
Que ha de mantener yacentes,
Más allá de bulla y corro,

A los cansados, sin fin
Vacación en los remotos
Jardines favorecidos
Por aquel interno otoño . . .

¡Imperen mal y dolor!
En mi semblante un sonrojo
De inaptitud se colore.
No cedo, no me abandono.

The morning's dismay
That whitens the prison close,
The emaciate quicklime
On monotonous walls,

And always plain to the sight, air's
Amplitude, on the other side of the locks,
And always, parched in our mouth,
Such bitter soliloquy . . .

That instant of weariness
Fallen to dreaming, in the calm
That must cherish some vacancy always
Beyond riot and tattle,

For the outwearied ones – sabbath
Unending, in the most inaccessible
Gardens, propitious
To autumns that come from within . . .

Anguish and wickedness thrive?
So be it! See how my impotence
Stands up in my eyes! I blush for it now.
I do not surrender. I do not make over.

III

Si las furias de un amor,
Si un paraíso de apóstol
¡Ay! me conducen —en nombre
De algún dios— hasta algún foso,

Si el combate, si el disturbio
Me desmenuzan en trozos
El planeta y se me clavan
Los añicos entre escombros,

Desde el centro del escándalo
Yo sufriré con los rotos.
Y cuando llegue la noche,
Astros habrá tan notorios

Que no fallará a mis plantas
El suelo. Yo me compongo
Para mi soberanía
La paz de un islote propio.

¿Quién podría arrebatarme
Tal libertad? No hay estorbo
Que al fin me anule este goce
Del más salvado tesoro.

III

If the rages of love,
The Eden of all the apostles –
God help me ! – should lead, in the name
Of some god – to the brink of some pit,

If the grappling, the muddlement
Should smite down a planet
And grind all to pieces, the smithereens
Splinter me fast in the rubble,

From the center of outrage
I will groan with the broken.
And when night has come down to us,
The stars in their places will show

Such a palpable concourse in heaven
That the earth will be firm to my stance. I elect
For my portion the beholden
Repose of an island atoll in the sea.

Who would wring from my grasp
So much liberty? No stumbling-stone
Under heaven will deny me that grace
Of securest largess, in the end.

IV

Si, cuando me duele el mundo,
En el corazón un pozo
Se me hundiera hacia el abismo
De esa Nada que yo ignoro,

Si los años me tornasen
Crepúsculo de rastrojo,
Si al huir las alegrías
Revolvieran su decoro,

Si los grises de los cerros
Me enfriasen los insomnios
Con sus cenizas de lunas
En horizontes de polvo,

¿Se sentiría vencido,
Apagado aquel rescoldo
De mi afán por las esencias
Y su resplandor en torno?

Heme ante la realidad
Cara a cara. No me escondo,
Sigo en mis trece. Ni cedo
Ni cederé, siempre atónito.

IV

True; when I wince for the world
I descend in that well of my heart
To the utter abysm
Of the Nothing I know nothing of.

And if years in their passing
Are as stubble and chaff in the night,
Or delights, evanescing,
Overturn their decorum,

Or high places empty their squalls
Binding my wakefulness
In the cinder and freeze of the moon
In horizons of ash —

Shall the coal of that rage
For the essences declare itself spent,
Or the splendors that compass it round
Own themselves darkened?

Myself and the actual, face to face —
It is well. I intend no concealment.
My belief does not waver. I do not make over.
I cede nothing over, forever astonished.

V

Lo sé. Horas volverán
Con su cabeza de toro
Negro asomándose, brusco,
Al camino sin recodo.

Vendrán hasta mi descanso,
Entre tantos repertorios
De melodías, las ondas
En tropeles inarmónicos.

¡Que se quiebre en disonancias
El azar! Creo en un coro
Más sutil, en esa música
Tácita bajo el embrollo.

El acorde —tan mordido,
Intermitente, recóndito—
Sobrevive y suena más.
Yo también a él respondo.

En su entereza constante
Palpo el concierto que sólido
Permanece frente a mí
Con el arco sin adorno.

V

I know it. They come back to us,
The hours with the head of a bull
Showing black and barbaric
On the point-blank approaches.

The tides of disharmony
Will move through my sleep
Tempestuously, borne
Among chanting assemblies.

Let calamity break, if it must,
Into dissonance! I affirm a more
Delicate singing, a reticent music
Of singers under all that rings false.

A concord – intermittent,
Diminished, and recondite –
Outsinging all others, that resonates **further**.
I answer that, too, in my kind.

And touch, in a timeless entirety,
The measures that rise to me here
And have in their keeping the palpable
Arch's unblemished simplicities.

¿Perdura el desbarajuste?
Algo se calla más hondo.
¿Siempre chirría la Historia?
De los silencios dispongo.

¿Y el inmediato prodigio
Que se me ofrece en su colmo
De evidencia? Yo me dejo
Seducir. —Ten ya mi elogio.

Entre tantos accidentes
Las esencias reconozco,
Profundas hasta su fábula.
Nada más real que el oro.

Así sueño frente a un sol
Que nunca me hallará absorto
Por dentro de algún celaje
Con reservas de biombos.

¿Marfil? Cristal. A ningún
Rico refugio me acojo.
Mi defensa es el cristal
De una ventana que adoro.

VI

¿Mientras, el mal? Fatalmente
Desordenando los modos
Guarde en su puño la cólera,

But bedlam persists, nonetheless?
Something deeper elects to be silent.
And History squeaks out of tune to us
Always? I order the silences.

And the immediate marvel
That proffers its warrant of plenitude –
What of that? I offer myself
To seduction. Have now my praises!

Amidst so great contingency
I acknowledge the essences,
Subtle as fable.
How actual is gold!

That way I dream in a sun
That never will show me distracted
In cloud wrack or sunburst
Through a screen's circumspection.

Ivory, then? Crystalline! No splendor's
Asylum can shelter me now.
My defenses are crystalline –
The glass of a window I cherish.

VI

Meanwhile – what of evil? Fatefully
Wrecking the symmetries,
Let it keep in its fist all ferocity,

Contraiga el visaje torvo,
Palpite con los reflejos
Cárdenos de los horóscopos,
Lleve la dicha hasta el ímpetu
Con que yo también acoso . . .
Necesito que una angustia
Posible cerque mis gozos
Y los mantenga en el día
Realísimo que yo afronto.
Rompa así la realidad
En mis rompientes y escollos,
Circúndeme un oleaje
De veras contradictorio,
Y en el centro me sitúe
De la verdad.
         ¿Alboroto?
Él me procura mi bien.
Difícil, sí, lo ambiciono,
¡Gracias!
         Continua tensión
Va acercándome a un emporio
De formas que ya diviso.
Con ellas avanzo, próspero.
¿Lo demás? No importe.
            Siga
Mi libertad al arroyo
Revuelto y dure mi pacto,
A través de los más broncos
Accidentes, con la esencia:

Tighten what's grim in our faces,
Shake with the darkened
Reflex of our horoscopes,
And carry our luck to abandonment's edge,
As I harry my happiness, too . . .
Some conceivable anguish
Must come within range of my pleasure
To nourish my joys
On that realest of days I confront.
Let me shatter reality so,
On my own reefs and my own shallows,
Encompass myself in their breaking successions
In true incongruity,
And there, in the center, stand fast
In my verity.
                    Confusions?
They win me the good that I will.
Intractable? Yes – I would have it so,
Thank you!
                    The stresses flow forward
Delivering into my hands
All the custom of forms that I fashion.
I go on with them, opulent.
And what of the rest?
                              That cannot matter.
My freedom follows a streaming
Return, my covenant stands
With the essences, among
Brutalest hazard.

Virtud radiante, negocio
De afirmación, realidad
Inmortal y su alborozo.
Para el hombre es la hermosura.
Con la luz me perfecciono.
Yo soy merced a la hermosa
Revelación: este Globo.
Se redondea una gana
Sin ocasos y me arrojo
Con mi avidez hacia el orbe.
¡Lo mucho para lo poco!
Es el orbe quien convoca.
¡Tanta invitación le oigo!
El alma quiere acallar
Su potencia de sollozo.
No soy nadie, no soy nada,
Pero soy —con unos hombros
Que resisten y sostienen
Mientras se agrandan los ojos
Admirando cómo el mundo
Se tiende fresco al asombro.

Virtue's effulgence, affirmation's
Exchanges, the eternally
Real, with its joys.
Man's portion is comeliness.
I make myself perfect with light.
I am graced with a fair
Revelation: the Globe of the world.
Inexhaustible longings surround me
And cast me forth into the dazzle
With all my avidities on me.
So much, for so little!
A planet assembles us.
I hear vast supplications.
The spirit would stay, if it could,
Its lamenting prerogative.
I am nobody! I am nothing at all!
But I am! Am one with all others
Whose shoulders resist and sustain
While their eyeballs grow great in their heads
And their wonderment cries that the world
Opens afresh to the onlooking ones.

BEN BELITT

CHRONOLOGY
of the Life and Work of Jorge Guillén

CHRONOLOGY
of the Life and Work of Jorge Guillén

1893   18 January. Birth of Pedro Jorge José Guillén, son of Julio Guillén and Esperanza Álvarez de Guillén, in Valladolid, Old Castile.

1903-1909   Secondary education at the Institute of Valladolid.

1909-1911   In Fribourg, Switzerland, at the Maison Perreyve of the French Fathers of the Oratory, from October 1909 to February 1911.

1911-1913   Enrolled in the Faculty of Philosophy and Letters at the Residencia de Estudiantes in Madrid.

1913   September. Receives Master of Arts degree from the University of Granada.

1913-1914   In Germany at Halle and Munich until 31 July 1914.

1914-1917   Madrid and Valladolid.

1917-1923   Lecturer in Spanish at the Sorbonne.

1918   Paris. Writes first poems.

1919   Begins writing *Cántico* during the summer in the village of Tregastel on the coast of Brittany.

1921   17 October. Marriage to Germaine Cahen in Paris.

1922   28 December. Birth of daughter Teresa in Paris.

1923   17 September. Death of mother in Valladolid.

1924   Receives Doctor of Letters degree from the University of Madrid.

2 September. Birth of son Claudio in Paris.

1925   Passes examinations for professorship in Madrid, and appointed professor at the University of Murcia.

1926-1929   Professor of Spanish Literature at the University of Murcia.

1928   First edition of *Cántico*, containing 75 poems, published in Madrid by Revista de Occidente.

1929-1931   Lecturer in Spanish at Oxford University.

1931-1938   Professor at the University of Seville.

1936   September. Jailed as political prisoner in Pamplona.

Second edition of *Cántico*, enlarged to 125 poems, published in Madrid by Cruz y Raya.

1938-1939   Professor at Middlebury College.

1939-1940   Professor at McGill University.

1940-1957   Professor at Wellesley College.

1945   Third edition of *Cántico*, with 270 poems, published in Mexico City by Litoral.

1947   Visiting professor at Yale University.

23 October. Death of Germaine in Paris.

1949   Summer in Valladolid; begins writing *Clamor*.

1950   1 April. Death of father in Valladolid.

September-December. Professor at the Colegio de México in Mexico City.

Fourth edition of *Cántico* (the first complete edition), containing 334 poems, published in Buenos Aires by Editorial Sudamericana.

1951   Visiting professor at the University of California at Berkeley.

Travel in Europe.

4 December. Death of poet Pedro Salinas in Boston.

1952   Visiting professor at Ohio State University.

1954   Summer in Italy.

Awarded Guggenheim Fellowship.

1955 In France, Minorca and Italy.

Receives Award of Merit of the American Academy of Arts and Letters.

1957 Appointed Charles Eliot Norton Professor of Poetry at Harvard University for 1957-1958.

Awarded the Poetry Prize of the City of Florence.

Maremágnum, the first part of *Clamor*, published in Buenos Aires by Editorial Sudamericana.

1958 June. Professor Emeritus, Wellesley College.

1958-1959 In Greece, Spain, France and Italy.

1959 Awarded the Etna-Taormina Poetry Prize, Sicily.

1960 In the United States, Puerto Rico and Italy.

... *Que van a dar en la mar*, the second part of *Clamor*, published in Buenos Aires by Editorial Sudamericana.

1961 January-July. In Italy.

Awarded Grand Prix International de Poésie, Ve Biennale de Knokke-Le Zoute, Belgium.

August-November. In Bogotá at the University of the Andes.

11 October. Marriage to Irene Mochi-Sismondi in Bogotá.

Expanded version of the Charles Eliot Norton lectures, *Language and Poetry: Some Poets of Spain*, published in Cambridge by Harvard University Press.

1962   Visiting professor at the University of Puerto Rico.

1963   In Italy and the United States.

The final part of *Clamor*, *A la altura de las circunstancias*, published in Buenos Aires by Editorial Sudamericana.